# Potential Impacts of the New Global Financial Architecture on Poor Countries

**Charles C. Soludo**
**Musunuru S. Rao**

## Monograph Series

The CODESRIA Monograph Series is published to stimulate debate, comments, and further research on the subjects covered. The Series will serve as a forum for works based on the findings of original research, which however are too long for academic journals but not long enough to be published as books, and which deserve to be accessible to the research community in Africa and elsewhere. Such works may be case studies, theoretical debates or both, but they incorporate significant findings, analyses, and critical evaluations of the current literature on the subjects in question.

Printed by Lightning Source

CODESRIA Monograph Series

ISBN-13: 978-2-86978-158-0

CODESRIA would like to express its gratitude to African Governments, the Swedish Development Co-operation Agency (SIDA/SAREC), the International Development Research Centre (IDRC), OXFAM GB/I, the Mac Arthur Foundation, the Carnegie Corporation, the Norwegian Ministry of Foreign Affairs, the Danish Agency for International Development (DANIDA), the French Ministry of Cooperation, the Ford Foundation, the United Nations Development Programme (UNDP), the Rockefeller Foundation, the Prince Claus Fund and the Government of Senegal for support of its research, publication and training activities.

# Contents

# List of boxes

# Summary

This monograph evaluates the potential impacts of the proposals for a new global financial architecture (NGFA) on poor countries and poor people. The mainstream proposals—put forth largely by the U.S., the G-7 countries and the Bretton Woods Institutions—are rooted in the neo-Walrasian, market fundamentalist view of the world, with the obvious consequence of increasing the vulnerabilities of small and poorer developing countries to frequent financial crises. It is shown that the claim of this model that global growth and equity would be 'best' served by deeper financial integration through open capital accounts is founded on shaky theoretical and empirical grounds. The model of premature and complete liberalization of the capital account in the context of endemic poverty, under developed and weak markets and institutions, and little or no formal social safety nets (e.g. unemployment and social insurance), is shown to exacerbate the vulnerability of small open (especially low-income) economies to disruptive and costly crises without any tangible benefits. Over time, this exposure could be growth retarding, as the devastating effects of shocks can be permanent especially on the poor, women and children. Most of the alternative proposals are rooted in the extreme institutionalist perspectives and call for new and stronger global governance structures. The alternative proposals seem overly optimistic, as the political support for establishing a 'global federal government' or other new global governance institutions in the near future might be lacking. Under the circumstances, a second-best approach with 'modifications' to the existing model may be pragmatic. It might entail a multi-speed or 'variable geometry' approach that takes into account the country circumstances and specific preconditions for sequencing of liberalization, including permissible 'speed-bumps' that countries can erect to avert crises.

Beside the overall framework of the reforms, the book shows that the specific proposals signal that the poorer developing countries are slated for more intrusive and pernicious doses of conditionalities, which, as under the structural adjustment programs prescribed by the Bretton Woods institutions, largely ignore local conditions and people's aspirations. On the other hand, the new architecture attempts to impose on poor countries (almost overnight) the Anglo-American corporate governance codes and standards, which have taken centuries to evolve. It is not clear that these codes and standards are necessarily well suited to meet the needs of low-income countries or would produce the promised results. However, the potential financial costs of their implementation can be enormous. Already, the various 'standards' agreed to at the WTO are costing these countries hundreds of millions of dollars to implement, and many are unable to meet the costs. The new doses of 'standards' required to be adopted under the new architecture add to the financial strain of these poor countries. Without external grants and technical assistance, the cash-strapped governments of poor countries might be forced to resort to diverting their meager budgetary allocations to the social and services sectors (e.g. education and health) and the environment, to comply with the demands of the IMF to compile and disseminate timely statistics.

Arguably, the most portent 'systemic risk' facing the global economy is not the threat of financial crisis but the endemic and deepening poverty. Ironically, the poor developing countries—home to more than 4 billion people—are largely excluded from the dialogue/discussions and decisions leading to the new architecture. This exclusion not only raises questions about the legitimacy of the new architecture, but also risks ignoring the most important issues germane to an effective and inclusive architecture. Furthermore, a number of issues of interest to the poor countries are missing in the existing proposals. Although the moral hazard problems of private creditors are addressed in the new architecture, those of the official creditors are left out. There is no discussion of a program to make the poor developing countries safe and attractive (profitable) for development of viable and vibrant financial systems and stem the massive tides of capital flight from these countries. Also missing are proposals to erect a truly transparent global financial system that would make money 'plundering' and 'laundering' unsafe anywhere. Without these and other key elements, the new architecture may confine deepening poverty and destitution in certain geographic boundaries and prosperity in others, leading to an ever widening gap between rich and poor countries and peoples.

Also, there is no program to systematically reconcile the imperatives of the new architecture with the internationally agreed goals and targets adopted at the World Summit for Social Development in Copenhagen (1995). Some of the recent add-on initiatives that complement the new architecture, especially the 'Enhanced Heavily Indebted Poor Countries (HIPC) Initiative' and conversion of the IMF's concessional lending facility (Enhanced Structural

Adjustment Facility or ESAF) into the Poverty Reduction and Growth Facility (PRGF) aimed at directly addressing poverty issues are welcome steps. They represent an attempt to 'do something' about poverty and are consistent with recent official rhetoric. However, it is unclear as to whether they would be ad-hoc or concerted; and would have adequate depth and resources to make significant and systematic impacts on poverty reduction.

# 1

# Introduction

> We cannot adopt a system in which the macroeconomic and financial is considered apart from the structural, social and human aspects and vice versa. Integration of each of these subjects is imperative at the national level and among the global players... the international financial architecture must reflect the interdependence of macro-economic and financial, with structural and social and human concerns... unless we adopt this approach on a comprehensive, transparent and accountable basis, we will fail in the global challenge of equitable and sustainable development and poverty alleviation. We will fail to build a sustainable international architecture for the coming millennium (Wolfensohn 1999).

It often takes a major shock to elicit a fundamental reform, and the East Asian currency and financial crises of the late 1990s have jolted the world into the long overdue reforms of the global financial system. While the causes of the crisis remain the subject of intense debate, most analysts agree that the global economy cannot afford a repeat of the vast and systemic disruptions that occurred. In just 1997 alone capital outflows from the emerging markets of Asia amounted to 11 percent of the countries' combined GDP, leaving in its wake an unspeakable human toll. More than 13 million people lost their jobs; real wages fell sharply by between 40 and 60 percent; bankruptcies spread; social spending on education and health suffered; the social fabric was seriously threatened with increased social unrest, crimes, violence in the home, etc. These impacts, especially on the social sectors, are likely to be long lasting.

The issue therefore is not whether, but what kinds of, reforms would not only prevent such crises in the future but more so deliver shared prosperity around the world. Given the nature of developments so far, this question might appear trite, as a new architecture is already being erected in the image of Washington and driven by the G-7 countries (with some consultations with the 12 to 20 major emerging markets). While there is a burgeoning literature and myriad proposals from all over the world for a new GFA, it is fair to say that the 'proposals' from Washington (U.S Treasury, IMF, and the World Bank) supported by the G-7, constitute the basis for the new GFA. Already, several aspects of the new GFA are being implemented (e.g. creation of the Forum for Financial Stability or FSF, new facilities of the IMF including the Contingent Credit Line or CCL, etc.). While the nuts and bolts of many aspects are still being worked out, an edifice with concrete shape is emerging. Essentially, these proposals are designed to strengthen and deepen the process of globalization already in place, which has been developed and reinforced through the harmonization of policies under the IMF/World Bank structural adjustment programs (SAPs) and the WTO rules on trade and investment. The emphasis has been on producing a public good—an improved global financial system—not only to ensure the stability and deeper integration of the financial systems, but also the internationalization (harmonization) of operational codes and standards.

The problem with every such exercise is that it caters primarily to the interests of the currently significant actors in the global markets (i.e. the OECD countries and the 12 to 20 systemically significant emerging market economies). The concerns of the other outliners are often problematic. Currently more than 100 countries and a few billion people, whose economies are rudimentary and poverty-stricken, are largely by-passed by the trends in the global capital markets, although these countries and their peoples are severely affected by the consequences. Some of the interests of these countries and their peoples are only footnoted in much of the current proposals, and are limited primarily to the need to care for the poor and vulnerable groups during crises.[1]

More fundamentally, the new Washington model of global financial reform makes a bold claim 'to build an international financial system that *best* promotes *global growth*, that contributes to a *broad-based sharing* in the benefits of that growth, and that is *less prone* to crises and better equipped to deal with crises when they occur' (Rubin 1999, emphasis added). In other words, the proposals and the emerging architecture are the 'best' that the world can have in order to address the development challenges of the Twenty-first century. The veracity of such a claim needs serious scrutiny. Thus, by what it contains and leaves out, the new architecture would have major impacts on poor countries and poor people. A fundamental but largely ignored issue is the consistency of the evolving architecture with the global aspiration (and imperative) of poverty eradication and the achievement of development targets adopted by more than 100 world leaders at the World Summit for Social Development (Copenhagen, March 1995) and by the OECD–World Bank and the United

Nations agencies. Unfortunately, there is little discussion or assessment of such impacts in the new architecture.

This monograph aims to accomplish three interrelated tasks: take issue with the claim that the framework of the new architecture is the 'best' to deliver equitable and rapid growth globally; draw attention to the potential impacts of the proposals on poor countries and peoples; and most importantly, highlight some of the missing pillars of the emerging structure which might be critical in ensuring a broad-based sharing in the benefits of global financial integration.

The rest of the monograph is organized as follows: Chapter 2 summarizes the highlights of the proposals, noting in particular the aspects that target the poor. In Chapter 3, the framework underlying the new architecture is critically evaluated. Chapter 4 explores the potential impacts of the proposals in the framework. In Chapter 5, attention is drawn to the missing agenda in the context of designing a socially inclusive architecture, while Chapter 6 incorporates some conclusions.

# 2

# Rationale and Overview of the New Global Financial Architecture

The crises of the decade have exposed the inadequacies of the existing system and highlighted the need for reforms. Traditionally, persistent deficits in the current account of the balance of payments often gave rise to financial crises. The jurisdiction and surveillance of the IMF was limited to the macroeconomic aspects that gave rise to these imbalances. The IMF's functions and the international financial system were designed at a time of public sector dominance. However, recent experiences show that financial crises could be triggered by other factors even when the macroeconomic fundamentals are sound. Popular explanations of the recent crises point to two other factors—the increasing dominance of the private sector in international financial markets, and the rapid movements of private capital at the first sign of either real or perceived trouble due to inadequate assessment of risks.

## Rationale

Over the years, the global financial system has become much more complex, with diverse actors—portfolio investors, commercial banks, and bondholders. The increasing sophistication of the system generates increased pressures for broader and more effective instruments for surveillance, monitoring and supervision of financial markets. It is thus argued that for more effective supervision and surveillance, there is a need for transparency, harmonization or internationalization of standards and codes, as well as the involvement of the private sector in dealing with crises. This has been the rationale for the nature of the reforms in the evolving New Global Financial Architecture (NGFA).

With the foregoing rationale, the reform process has been driven by the G-7 Finance ministers and Central Bank Governors, the G-22 countries, and the Bretton Woods institutions. It has been 'agreed that the IMF should remain at the centre of the international monetary system, while improving in a pragmatic manner the modus operandi of its institutional components and co-operation with other institutions and fora'.[2]

## Objective

The objective of the reforms is to strengthen the efficiency and stability of global financial integration. According to Camdessus (1999a:4), 'the goal, summarized in a very few words, is to build a sounder international system that is conducive to free, but orderly, international capital movements, based on sound national systems and prudent, transparent macroeconomic policymaking'. Corroborating this, the G-7 ministers of Finance stress that 'these reforms are designed to: increase the transparency and openness of the international financial system; identify and disseminate international principles, standards and codes of best practice; strengthen incentives to meet these international standards; and strengthen official assistance to help developing countries reinforce their economic and financial infrastructure. They also include policies and processes to ensure the stability and improve the surveillance of the international financial system. Finally, they aim at reforming the International Financial Institutions, such as the IMF, while deepening co-operation among industrialized and developing countries'.

### Main Elements of the NGFA

The main elements of the proposals as summarized by the IMF are as follows:[3]

*Transparency, Standards and Surveillance*[4]

The basic objective of transparency is to help foster better decision-making and economic performance by improving transparency in the policies and practices of member countries and international institutions. On the one hand, the IMF's role is to encourage member countries to be more transparent and, on the other, become more transparent about IMF policies and advice to members. The latter included making available more information on IMF surveillance of member countries, IMF-supported programs of the countries, IMF analyses of country policy issues, members' financial accounts with the Fund and the Fund's liquidity position, and information from the private sector. Enhancing the consultative process on the HIPC Initiative, and strengthening the supervisory/regulatory structures and disclosure for highly leveraged institutions also formed a part of the package.

5

The basic objective on standards is to 'foster the development, dissemination, and adoption of internationally accepted standards or codes of good practice for economic, financial, and business activities'.[5] The proposals include the strengthening of the Special Data Dissemination Standards (SDDS) developed by the IMF in 1996; and developing standards, by appropriate standard-setting institutions, on such aspects as accounting and auditing, bankruptcy, corporate governance, insurance regulations, payment and settlement systems, and securities market regulations, that are relevant for the efficient functioning of the financial systems. Also, it included codes of good practices on monetary and financial policies and on fiscal policies. Improvements in the quality of bank supervision internationally were also emphasized. Lastly, it was proposed that social policies should be strengthened as an essential complement to the reform of the international financial system.

The basic objective of surveillance is to strengthen the incentives for adoption of the international standards. The proposals include better integration of the use of the standards in Fund surveillance reports, move toward comprehensive reporting on the capital account to better assess capital flows and external vulnerability, and develop an early warning system for balance of payments crises.

*Strengthening Financial Systems*

The basic objective is to further strengthen the financial systems. The Fund's role is to contribute to the strengthening, development, and dissemination of international principles and good practices of sound financial systems; strengthen its surveillance of countries' financial systems, and support jointly with the World Bank structural reforms to strengthen the financial sectors. The proposals include improved financial market supervision, improved collaboration between the Fund and the Bank in strengthening financial systems, and increased focus of Fund surveillance on the links between macroeconomic policies and banking system soundness.

*Orderly Integration of International Financial Markets*

The basic objective is to allow countries reap the benefits of financial integration, including capital account liberalization, while carefully managing the process to reduce risks. The IMF's role is to investigate the ways in which it might best foster the orderly integration of international financial markets. The role of capital controls in the orderly integration is also to be considered.

*Mobilizing the Private Sector*

The objective is to involve the private sector in crisis prevention and crisis resolution, in order to limit moral hazard, strengthen market discipline, and help bring about orderly adjustment when crises occur, while maintaining international financial flows. The IMF is to join with the international community to assess and advance specific proposals for involving the private sector in the prevention and resolution of financial crises. The proposals include measures to raise the cost of short-term cross-border capital flows, encourage countries to arrange commercial contingent credit lines, embed call options in inter-bank loan agreements, organize creditor-debtor councils, expand dialogue with the private sector, encourage changes in terms of foreign sovereign bond contracts, lend into sovereign arrears to private bondholders and non-sovereign arrears arising from exchange controls during debt negotiations, and provide for the imposition of stays on creditor litigation to facilitate orderly non-sovereign debt renegotiations.

*Systemic Aspects*

The objective is to strengthen the international monetary system to better cater to the profound changes in recent years. The IMF would adapt its financial facilities, resources, and its organization to the evolving international monetary system. The proposals include the provision of contingent credit lines (CCLs) by the IMF, increase in the Fund's quotas, bring into force the New Arrangements to Borrow, and allow for the special one-time allocation of SDRs. Also, it was proposed to secure full financing for the interim ESAF and the Fund's participation in the HIPC Initiative. Finally, it was proposed to strengthen and/ or transform the Interim Committee of the Fund into a Council.

## Assessment

It is a comprehensive list of proposals that may overtax the capacities of at least some developed countries, possibly many developing countries, and no doubt all poor countries. Action on a majority of the proposals is underway. However, the main exceptions are in the area of mobilization of the private sector. Also, action on a few proposals impinging on the systemic aspects are yet to be taken. Overall, the proposals and actions seem to strengthen/ reinforce the central role of the IMF. They incorporate iterative improvements on the traditional policies and practices of the Fund with a few new roles, responsibilities, and instruments added to its existing complement. The emerging structure largely driven by the IMF appears to be intended to further strengthen the role of the IMF in the international financial system.

At the time of its establishment in 1945, the IMF was seen as the major actor in facilitating the orderly functioning of the international financial system. However, by the 1990s, private sector actors have become dominant in the system with transactions that dwarf the flows from IMF and other official sources. The emerging structure seems to lay undue emphasis on the apparent factors that contributed to the East Asian crisis and does not appear to respond adequately to the other changed circumstances. It is driven by the 'new Washington Consensus' on international development. In the process, a major opportunity to rethink the structure of international finance and global economic governance based on full participation of all countries and incorporating pluralistic perspectives seemed to be lost.

## Standards, Codes, Principles and Regulations

As mentioned in the previous sub-section, a plethora of standards, codes, principles and regulations are being advanced for adoption by all countries to avert and/or ameliorate the impact of major financial crises. The more significant of these are listed below:

- a strengthened version of the Special Data Dissemination Standards (SDDS) developed by the IMF in 1966. Its objective is to guide countries that have or might seek access to international capital markets in the provision of their economic and financial data to the public;
- a code of good practices on fiscal transparency developed by the IMF. It incorporates principles that espouse clarity of roles and responsibilities of the various levels of government and public entities, public availability of information, open budget preparation, execution and reporting, and public and independent scrutiny of the fiscal information;
- a draft code of good practices on monetary and financial policies developed recently under the leadership of the IMF;
- core principles for effective bank supervision developed under the leadership of the Basle Committee for Bank Supervision (BCBS);
- objectives and principles of securities regulation and disclosure standards to facilitate cross-border offering and initial listings by multinational issuers

endorsed by the International Organization of Securities Commissions (IOSCO);

- a comprehensive set of International Accounting Standards promulgated by the International Accounting Standards Committee (IASC) and the core standards drawn from these to be recommended by IOSCO to be used by foreign issuers in cross-border listings and offerings;
- a set of international standards on auditing and audit practice developed by the International Federation of Accountants (IFAC) to be adopted by foreign issuers for cross-border offerings, and to be considered for adoption by (developing) countries as national standards;
- insurance principles, standards and guidance papers and standards relating to licensing, on-site inspections and supervision of derivatives issued by the International Association of Insurance Supervisors (IAIS); good practices on corporate governance developed by the OECD, World Bank and the Basle Committee;
- bankruptcy laws, regulations and good practices being developed by the United Nations Commission on International Trade Law (UNCITRAL), World Bank and International Bar Association; improvements in the international payment systems being developed by the Committee on Payment and Settlements Systems; and
- general principles of good practices in social policy to be developed by the World Bank.

The above standards, codes, principles and regulations, for the most part, reflect the practices on the relevant aspects in the United States. The US wields a disproportionate influence in setting the new rules. For example, The US Securities and Exchange Commission (SEC) is a major actor in the work of IOSCO. Subscription to and compliance with many of these by the countries are indicated to be voluntary. The practices in most of the other developed countries do not fully conform to the standards, etc. However, negotiations have been underway recently to achieve some degree of uniformity and conformity on some of the standards, etc., among the developed countries. It is unclear as to how many developed countries would volunteer to refashion themselves in the mold of the US. At the same time, the risk is that the developing countries are being and/or would be coerced to adopt the standards, etc., as a condition for access to international financial markets and for continued assistance from international financial institutions (especially IMF and the World Bank) and some bilateral donors.

**Provisions Targeting Developing Countries and Poor People**

Beside the general principles discussed above, there are specific issues, which are tacked on to the proposals to underscore the all-inclusive nature of the architecture. The G-7 Declaration had noted that 'the reform of the international financial system is in the interest of all countries and all need to be involved in the process'. Several official pronouncements on the NGFA are consequently sprinkled with some specific 'recognitions' of the interests of the poor countries as well as proposals that ought to cater to their specific needs. Some of these include:

a)  recognition that the opening of capital markets in emerging economies must be carried out in a careful and well-sequenced manner if countries are to benefit from closer integration into the global economy. In particular, financial sectors and regulatory and supervisory regimes must be robust and adequate to deal with risk; and

b) agreement that more attention must be given in times of crisis to the effect of economic adjustment on the most vulnerable groups in society. The World Bank was mandated to develop as a matter of urgency general principles of good practice in social policy, in consultation with other relevant institutions. These should be drawn upon in developing adjustment programs in response to crisis. In particular, as Rubin (1999:6) suggested, 'there are several conclusions we can draw from the recent crisis as they apply to principles and practices of good social policy', which include:

    i)   maintaining a fiscal framework designed to protect core social expenditures at pre-crisis levels, or at least to prevent disproportionate reductions;

    ii)  designing means-tested programs for the poor and disadvantaged and developing effective and targeted programs for the most vulnerable;

    iii) strengthening anti-corruption measures, especially through fiscal transparency and accountability; and

    iv)  adhering to core labour standards.

So far, many of the proposals have been concretised and already being implemented. The Interim Committee, which was working on the proposals, issued a Communiqué at the end of September 1999 pointing out the progress made. The Committee noted that there was broad agreement on the importance of transparency, on the definition of global standards to underpin efficient, fair and stable markets, and on financial sector stability. Emphasis was shifting from the defining of standards to their dissemination, implementation, and monitoring.

But controversy lingers not only about the framework of the architecture itself, but also (and more so) about the details of the component proposals. As Camdessus (1999a) suggests, there is lack of consensus on at least three key issues. First, there is difficulty in designing a Washington Consensus style 'one-size-fits-all' approach to involving private sector in crisis prevention and resolution, especially given the widely differing circumstances. Second, there is controversy about the optimal rate of proceeding with liberalization of capital movements on the one hand and the role of direct exchange controls on the other. Third, there is debate about the implications of the crisis for the choice of exchange rate regimes in developing countries.

# 3

## Disputing the Framework
## of the New Architecture

### Underlying Development Model

At the fundamental level and for years to come, the most controversial aspect of the NGFA would pertain to its underlying model of the market economy ('view of the world'). So far, the debate has been conducted largely at two extremes, with a myriad of hybrid views in between. At one end of the spectrum is the market fundamentalist model, while at the other end, is the institutionalist view. The former identifies defects/crisis in the economy with 'distortions' induced by government intervention ('government failure') and concludes that the best response to a crisis is to remove the 'government distortions'. For the institutionalists, pervasive market failures (domestically and internationally) abound, and thus an appropriate response is 'more government' interventions. Reality however, might be somewhere in between as the world cannot be adequately described as 'either' white or black.

There is little debate that the market economy is the best framework for organizing economic activity yet discovered by mankind. Not many economists would defend communism as a better economic model. Rubin (1999:1) stressed this point by noting that 'our approach to reforming the global financial architecture is based on the fundamental belief that market-based systems create the best prospects for job creation, economic growth and rising living standards both in the United States and around the world'. But 'market-based systems' entail a rich variety of systems and models, each of which can conceivably also deliver prosperity. Beside the neo-classical theory, there are several other vintages such as neo-Keynesian, structuralist, and institutionalist perspectives. The diagnosis and policy prescriptions of each of the schools of thought, while within the market economy framework, can be significantly different. Furthermore, given the evident inter-dependencies among individual economies with strong cross-border spillover effects of shocks, not many economists would dispute the need for some form of coordination and/or harmonization of policies and procedures (multilateralism). The extent of such coordination or harmonization (deep versus shallow) is however controversial. Ultimately the choice of one model over the others depends on the beliefs and the political power wielded by any group at a point in time rather than on the relative superiority of one model over the other.[6]

Currently, the dominant political powers favour the market fundamentalist neo-classical model, albeit with some attempt to tack on a 'human face' or 'compassion' to it. Under this framework, there is an untenable drive to a unique world system wherein every economy should look alike. This model, which provides the framework for the new global financial architecture (NGFA), is rooted in six widely held but largely unsubstantiated assumptions regarding the imperatives of the global economy.[7] These are: (i) all countries should converge to one single (Anglo-American) model of capitalism; (ii) market fundamentalism—a neo-Walrasian view of the market in which the market is always efficient and all ills are blamed on the intrusive state—is the best means of organizing economic activity; (iii) free trade and unfettered mobility of financial resources (through capital account liberalization) are the best guarantees to broadly shared global prosperity; (iv) foreign investment is key to growth, employment generation, and technological progress in the developing countries; (v) growth would always trickle down to the poor and; (vi) if the proposals in the Washington-made NGFA are implemented, they would prevent future financial crises.

Derived basically from the neoclassical economic principles, this view of the world sees globalization as having greatly diminished the scope for national policies, and that the optimal response is to 'harmonize' public policies and corporate standards globally (i.e. internationalization of private and public behaviour). From this perspective the challenge facing the international community is to 'deepen' globalization (through the NGFA and WTO negotiations), while the task of national economies is simply to 'adapt' to the process. To be sure, these assumptions constitute a set of the mainstream view to the extent that they drive much of the current global economic policies and national reforms in developing countries. Being 'mainstream', however, is different from being 'right' or 'adequate' set of assumptions and policies to 'best' deliver broad-based global prosperity. We scrutinize the framework in terms of its appropriateness and adequacy, especially from the perspective of the poorest developing countries.

The logic of the model is simple. Financial integration (through liberalization) is an integral element of the globalization bandwagon. Like free trade, the free movement of financial resources 'allocates capital to its most productive uses across countries and allows residents to engage in welfare-improving inter-temporal consumption smoothing. In a competitive model with perfect foresight and complete markets, the welfare benefit from inter-temporal finance is identical to the welfare benefit from international trade in goods and services' (Dooley 1998:85). It is assumed that international capital markets price assets accurately according to the fundamentals. In this case, capital flows would transfer savings from areas with low marginal productivity investments to areas with higher productivity investments. Thus, free capital mobility allocates resources efficiently around the globe, thereby promoting investment and growth. Because of its reversibility, capital mobility also serves to 'discipline' governments and 'force' them to adopt sound fiscal and monetary policies. For the developing countries in particular, this phenomenon is expected to bring great benefits as they usually suffer acute shortage of investable resources (capital), just as the domestic financial liberalization under SAP was seen as a way to alleviate credit constraints while also improving resource allocation.

Needless to say that this laissez faire model requires some very strict conditions for it to obtain in practice. These include: no increasing returns, no monopolies, a complete set of well-operating markets for present and future goods, complete insurance markets, fully available and symmetric information, lump sum transfer payments, etc. (Kanbur and Lustig 1999:2).

This model, especially the neo-Walrasian view of the market, has underpinned much of the analysis of the causes of the East Asian crisis and the remedial prescriptions, much of which are now added to the NGFA. Under this framework, the market is efficient, and every problem in the economy must be associated with something the government has done 'wrong'.

## Critique of the Model

But neo-classical economics is neither the only economics nor a rocket science. Serious and persisting theoretical and empirical challenges continue to be mounted against the model and the assumptions discussed above.

For example, on a purely theoretical basis, the neo-classical claim about the efficiency of the financial system can be challenged. It is easy for the new Keynesian models of noise trading to show that in markets where traders ignore fundamentals, it is rational for even fundamentalists to jump on the speculative bandwagon and drive prices away from their underlying 'correct' levels. A more conventional Keynesian position is that no unique fundamentals exist in any case, since the correct asset price depends on the distribution of income, political power, and a host of other complex (unknown) factors. This would be consistent with the new models of exchange rate crisis which show that even in the face of neo-classical 'rationality', international capital markets have multiple equilibria; thus, if speculators attack, they can move the economy from a sustainable point to an inferior position (Baker *et al*. 1998:24).

Furthermore, economists such as Stiglitz, Akerlof, Greenwald, and others have also successfully challenged the model of perfect information and competitive markets. They show that in the presence of imperfect information or incomplete/missing markets, the market equilibria would not be Pareto efficient. The theoretical insights provided by Stiglitz, have now been accepted as part of the mainstream economics. As Kanbur and Lustig (1999:4) acknowledge, '... our argument is that one of the reasons inequality is back on the agenda is that the last two decades have culminated in a triumph of the imperfect information and imperfect markets perspective in mainstream economics'. Bryant (1999:2) corroborates this view, noting that completely unconstrained financial activity may not be able to deliver the promised benefits. This, according to him, is because of 'informational asymmetries, adverse selection and moral hazard, informational cascades, herding behaviour and contagion, and excessive volatility in asset prices cause financial activity to be inherently vulnerable to instability'.

Unfortunately, such valid theoretical propositions are still grudgingly treated as useful footnotes in the eminently neo-classical Washington Consensus. World Bank President Wolfensohn agrees in his paper (1999:4) from which we draw the opening quote for this monograph. He admits that, 'we know, at least from hindsight, that part of the failures in Russia were due to paying insufficient attention to the *preconditions* for a market economy. Too often in the past, we have gone after the 'easy' targets, saying that we would attack the more difficult (often institutional) issues later on. In doing so, we have failed to recognize the essential complementarities' (emphasis added). Similar *preconditions* are also missing in most of the poorest developing countries, and there is a danger that the evolving architecture would make the same mistakes. It is not surprising that with Stiglitz as the Chief Economist of the World Bank and Wolfensohn as President, the Bank has in recent times (at least in high profile

**15**

speeches and publications) admitted that the 'old Washington Consensus' was either wrong or grossly inadequate, and thus a need for a 'post-Washington Consensus'. Part of the new cliché is that 'institutions matter'. Getting the Bretton Woods institutions (BWIs) to acknowledge this point is a major triumph, but the more fundamental question is 'what kinds of institutions matter most for economies at certain levels of development, and how do we bring those about?' This is the heart of the matter. But ironically, it gets a short shrift in mainstream policy designs, recommendations and conditionalities of the BWIs.

The reason is a simple one. Traditions and ideologies die hard. It is believed that the World Bank and the IMF, with the current composition of their staff, are being asked to design and implement detailed institutional and structural reforms, which they neither have the training nor the experience to do. While Stiglitz and his followers might understand clearly the microeconomic underpinnings of market failures, the bulk of the staff of the BWIs are still wedded to the neo-classical macroeconomic principles. Thus, there is a big disjuncture between the 'recognition' of what needs to be done and its translation and incorporation in the operations of the institutions. At the limit, the staff simply take recourse to what they know best, namely, thinking of policies within the framework of perfectly competitive market models. Thus, the emerging 'new Washington Consensus' is simply the ad-hoc addition to the 'old Consensus' of such things as labour market flexibility (liberalization of labour markets including the freedom of firms to layoff workers), enhanced financial supervision and prudential regulation, transparency and good governance, and social safety nets. Predictably, the underlying model is still the neo-classical economic framework, and the goal of reforms continues to be to create perfectly competitive markets by removing all the 'distortions'.

This dogmatic bent has pervaded much of the diagnosis and policy package prescriptions of the BWIs to the Asian countries during the crisis, and also underpins the evolving new financial architecture. As to the causes of the crisis, the mainstream Washington position is that it was caused by crony capitalism, corruption, inadequate rule of law, lack of transparency, weak financial regulation and supervision, poor corporate governance, non-enforcement of bankruptcy procedures, an insufficiently open capital account, overly ambitious industrial policies, etc. Simply put, the crisis was interpreted as the result of 'distortions' in the market economy. For solutions, the $57 billion rescue package for South Korea carried a large set of conditions that could give insights into the nature of the evolving architecture. The more significant elements of the program included:

- tight monetary policies, higher interest rates, and a fiscal retrenchment initially equivalent to about 2 percent of GDP (the latter requirement was significantly relaxed in subsequent programs as the Korean economy deteriorated more than anticipated);
- a comprehensive financial-sector restructuring, including independence of the central bank and the suspension of the operations of nine merchant banks;
- the dismantling of 'nontransparent and inefficient ties among the government, banks, and businesses', including the phasing out of the system of cross guarantees within conglomerates;
- a program of trade liberalization, including the phasing out of trade-related subsidies, restrictive import licensing, and the import diversification program;
- capital-account liberalization, including the lifting of all capital-account restrictions on foreign investors' access to the Korean bond market; and
- labour market reforms, aimed particularly at making layoffs easier while enhancing social safety nets.

As Rodrik (1999a:6) puts it, 'the reforms in labor-market institutions, trade and capital accounts, and government-business relations entail a remolding of the Korean economy in the image of a Washington economist's idea of a free market economy. If Korea, a mid-size country with an exemplary development record, is subject to such intrusive conditionality, one can imagine what is in store for small countries with more checkered economic histories'. On the implications of the new conditionality, Rodrik (pp. 2–12) laments that:

> An unappreciated irony in this is that conditionality on developing countries is being ratcheted up at precisely the moment when our comprehension of how the global economy works and what small countries need to do to prosper within it has been revealed to be sorely lacking...Ignorance calls for humility...there are dangers in throwing at developing countries a Washington-consensus view of economic policy, even if this consensus is now refurbished with new international codes and standards and with 'second-generation reforms'... The reality is that our prescriptions often go considerably beyond what can be supported by careful theoretical reasoning or empirical demonstration... Economies that have done well in the postwar period have all succeeded

via their own particular brand of heterodox policies...So we have to entertain the idea that sound economic policy is not common knowledge, or that information sets about what constitutes sound economic policy differ... Today's developed countries did not get their regulatory and legal institutions overnight. It would be nice if third-world countries could somehow acquire first-world institutions, but the safe bet has to be that this will happen only when they are no longer third-world countries.

Many economists are certainly unhappy with both the neo-classical interpretation of the Asian crisis and the kinds of policy reforms (conditionalities) foisted upon these economies. For example, the fundamental cracks in the Washington Consensus could not be papered over as Stiglitz led an open combat against the IMF on the issues. Stiglitz (1998a) systematically disputes both the diagnosis of the causes of the East Asian crisis and the policy prescriptions, and makes a case for more systematic interventions in the economy by governments in contrast to the laissez-faire orthodoxy.

For Stiglitz, a major part of the policies that led up to the East Asia's vulnerability to crisis was the 'excessively' rapid financial (capital account) liberalization, and the 'inadequate financial regulation'. He observes that, in fact, 'some of the countries with the weakest financial sectors, the greatest lack of transparency, and the most corrupt political structures were hardly touched by the contagion from East Asia. These were countries with closed, or at least more closed, capital accounts' (p.4). 'Interestingly, in a country like Korea, financial liberalization was undertaken in no small part in response to U.S. pressure and to satisfy the requirements of OECD membership. This is indeed a poignant example of how ill-advised external pressure—grounded in partial economic theory and inadequate evidence (but solid mercantilist reasons)—can prove harmful to the recipient' (Rodrik 1999a:9).

Many other economists agree with Stiglitz. Volcker (1998:4) suggests that, 'the timing, nature, and force of the Asian financial crisis...[cannot] be explained in terms of those structural factors, important as they may be over time. None of them is new. None of them has been unknown nor, to the best of my knowledge, suddenly gotten worse'. In other words, the structural and institutional characteristics of an economy do not necessarily have to be of the Anglo-American vintage to prevent a financial crisis. Different models of market economy exist, with varieties of national characteristics, and they have not crashed as a consequence of financial turmoil. Indeed, as Feldstein (1998) who has trenchantly criticized the IMF's departure from its traditional roles into more intrusive structural details has observed, 'the specific policies that the IMF insists must be changed are not so different from those in the major countries of Europe: labor market rules that cause 12 percent unemployment, corporate ownership structures that give banks and governments controlling interests in industrial companies, state subsidies to inefficient and loss-making industries, and trade barriers that restrict Japanese auto imports to a trickle and block foreign purchase of industrial companies'.[8]

## Global Financial Governance

The major point of the foregoing discussion is that much of the analysis and prescription in the literature fail to recognize the fundamental defect of the global financial system, namely, its inherent instability, especially in the absence of effective governance institution. At the national level, governments seek to govern the financial system by insisting on: high standards for accounting, auditing, and information disclosure; well designed and competently administered legal procedures for enforcing contracts and adjudicating disputes; skilful prudential supervision and regulation of private financial institutions; an effective but limited potential for crisis management and crisis lending ('lender-of-last-resort' provisions); and, not least, sound and predictable macroeconomic environment for the financial system and wider economy to operate (Bryant 1999). The fact is that this kind of governance does not exist at the global level. 'There exists no world legal system, no infrastructure of international courts or legal bodies for the resolution of cross-border disputes… The world has only nascent supranational institutions, with very limited responsibilities for the prudential oversight of financial activity…' (Bryant, pp. 2-3). In effect, there is a basic asymmetry between the organization of economic activity at the national and global levels. Given the unique features of financial transactions and their inherent instability, strong governmental oversight is key to its stability and effectiveness. But this exists only at the national level. There are no supranational institutions responsible for sound global monetary and fiscal policies, and lender-of-last-resort institution—important prerequisites for global financial stability. Much of the current reforms are designed, in an ad-hoc manner, to respond to some of the shortcomings by recommending minimum global standards in the areas of accounting, auditing, data collection and dissemination. But they are not adequate to guarantee stability.

It is this search for stability of global finance that has led several analysts to propose 'radical' changes to the global collective governance structure—something akin to lender of last resort (world central bank), and stronger global governance (world federal government). For these proponents, only these institutions could play the analogous supervisory and management roles performed by the national institutions. As we have noted earlier, these proposals might be politically infeasible until at least several decades in the future.

## Critique of the NGFA Framework

Without effective global governance institutions, it is then intuitive that unfettered capital mobility, with all the vulnerabilities that go with it, may hardly deliver the expected broad-based growth its proponents expect. For countries at earlier stages of development, some forms of capital and financial controls might in fact be more growth enhancing. Williamson (1990:19) argues that there is 'relatively little support for the notion that liberalization of international capital flows is a priority objective for a country that should be a capital importer and ought to be retaining its own savings for domestic investment'. Thus, beside the issue of vulnerability to crisis, Williamson emphasizes the need for some controls so that developing countries can retain their savings for investment and hence growth. Stiglitz (1998a:5) corroborates this argument and argues, in fact, that neither theory nor evidence supports the mainstream claim that capital account liberalization leads to faster growth. According to him:

> the ideological position is that financial market liberalization is important because it also leads to faster economic growth, by reducing distortions in the market economy. But both empirical evidence and recent economic theory cast doubt on that proposition. There is evidence that economies that have engaged in mild financial restraints, such as moderate restrictions on interest rates—and that in so doing have increased the franchise value of their banks, enhancing the safety and soundness of the financial system—have, if anything, grown more quickly as a result. This evidence is consistent with theoretical studies that have shown that even increased capital requirements cannot efficiently offset the adverse incentives associated with diminished franchise values. Excessively rapid financial liberalization can, in fact, undermine the strength of financial systems, thereby reducing growth. Many observers attribute the apparent increase in the frequency and severity of financial crises, especially in developing countries, to the way in which financial liberalization has been carried out.

This represents a formidable challenge to the very foundations of the new architecture—based on the assumption that unfettered capital mobility is the 'best' way to ensure rapid and broadly shared global growth. The notion that capital account liberalization is always good for growth is not borne out by evidence. In theory, it is wrong to treat flows of goods and services the same

**20**

way as capital flows. The assumption only holds 'if' there are no market imperfections. But the truth is that financial markets suffer from various imperfections—informational asymmetries, agency problems, self-fulfilling expectations, bubbles, and myopia—and these make the markets inherently vulnerable to periodic crises. Worse still, 'no amount of institutional tinkering is likely to make a significant difference to that basic fact of life' (Rodrik 1999a:22). Thus, countries have to weigh the putative benefits from overly ambitious liberalization against the huge economic and social costs of potential crises which small open economies are vulnerable to (Lee 1998:16). And the impacts of such costs can be long lasting.

For example, 'we know now that the effects of unemployment and bankruptcy on the poorer half of the population can be permanent; in Mexico increases in child labor force participation and reduced enrolment in school during the 1995 downturn have not been reversed. Similarly a collapse in employment opportunities for labor force entrants can have lifetime effects on job possibility and income-earning potential for the affected cohorts' (Birdsall 1999:4). Furthermore, Rodrik (1998) compared the growth performance of countries with liberalized capital account and those that have not, and found no evidence that the former outperformed the latter. Instead, many countries with spectacular growth performances in recent history did so without open capital accounts; e.g. Japan in 1950s and 1960s; South Korea until recently; and China today. If open capital account has no proven benefits (countries can grow without it) but carries enormous risks of vulnerability to crises, it is not clear why it should be the central pillar of the new financial architecture. Thus, the very edifice of the new architecture has no strong root in theory or empirical evidence.

*What about stability?* Another claim of the proponents of the underlying model of the NGFA is that it would ensure 'stability' and hopefully 'prevent' future crises. Again, there is no strong theoretical or empirical basis for this claim. As indicated earlier, financial market for short-term debt (portfolio flows) is 'inherently unstable' because of the plethora of market imperfections discussed earlier. At the empirical level, countries like Sweden, Finland and Norway experienced severe financial crises in 1992–93, and even the most uncharitable analyst is not likely to attribute the so-called 'distortions' of corruption and crony-capitalism in Asian economies to these Nordic countries. Furthermore, at the beginning of the adjustment programs in the 1980s, one of the arguments for liberalization was that it guards against, or dampens the effects

**21**

of, external shocks/crises. Ironically, the East Asian countries that were the exemplar outward-oriented economies, turned out to be the ones most hit by the crisis while the relatively 'closed' economies avoided it. As a general fact of life, Stiglitz (p.1) cautions that: 'even with the best economic management, small open economies remain vulnerable. They are like small rowboats on a wild and open sea. Although we may not be able to predict it, the chances of eventually being broadsided by a large wave are very significant no matter how well the boat is steered'. Such is the plight of small open economies in Africa, Asia and Latin America. Unfortunately, this point is sorely missed in the proposals emanating from Washington for a new architecture.

Bearing in mind the inherent vulnerability of small open economies to crisis, Stiglitz (pp.8-9) calls for greater humility and caution in pushing policy reforms:

> We cannot expect to eliminate all fluctuations or all crises. Even if we could eliminate all the 'problems' and 'mistakes' in economic policy, it is unlikely that we could fully insulate economies against shocks, including events such as the OPEC oil price increases in the 1970s or changes in market sentiment, such as occurred in the current East Asian crisis. Furthermore, although there is much more scope for policy reforms in developing countries, we should not delude ourselves into thinking that this can take place over night. Building robust financial systems is a long and difficult process. In the meantime, we need to be realistic and recognize that developing countries have less capacity for financial regulation and greater vulnerability to shocks. We need to take this into account in policy recommendations in all areas, especially in the timing and sequencing of opening up capital markets to the outside world and in the liberalization of the financial sector... I think that the time is ripe for an open debate and discussion on the advantages and limitations of a variety of approaches, including some form of taxes, regulations, or restraints on international capital flows.

This cautionary note and call for open debate and pragmatism is consistent with the views of a growing number of economists. Whether and how these powerful views would make it into the NGFA that seems to be almost foreclosed remains to be seen.

The final half-truth that underlies the model of the new architecture and indeed the globalization process is the drive towards the 'harmonization' of national institutional and structural characteristics into one global model of market economy. Such harmonization is often justified on the grounds of deeper integration of the global economy. There is, implicit in this logic, something like a 'federal global economic space'. This is a myth, and indeed, objectionable for a number of reasons.

First, despite the waves of globalization, national economic borders are not likely to disappear any time soon. Indeed, most economic activities still exhibit significant 'home bias'—with more than 90 percent of domestic investment determined by domestic savings; capital mobility between the rich and poor countries is not anywhere near what could be predicted by theoretical models and even the minuscule flows are concentrated in only a dozen countries; international price arbitrage in tradable commodities occurs very slowly; and not to mention that restrictions on labor mobility is the rule. So, the integration process is not as deep as proclaimed. Indeed, some analysts point out that aside from the character of globalization (in terms of breath-taking changes in technologies, and transport and communications), the extent of integration of the markets for goods and finance is not much different from what it was at the beginning of the century.

Second, there is, and will in the foreseeable future continue to be, a disjuncture between global economics and politics. In so far as population (and labor) is confined to geographic locations and politics remains localized, the drive towards 'one' model of market economy will continue to be elusive. When pushed to the extreme, local politicians would ultimately pander to their electorate. Malaysia is trying an experiment, which may well set the tone for others. Recent election of left-of-centre governments in the major countries of Europe—U.K., Germany, France, etc.—led to the modification of the Maastricht criteria to include employment (and social) targets. These are clear examples of how domestic politics will continue to come into conflict with globalization or mono-economics. What the global system probably needs is a rule-based multilateral system to ensure global stability. In this way, Moslems would be allowed to continue to be Moslems,[9] the French can continue to be French, Asians to be themselves, etc. This is very different from the current approach of free trade and open capital accounts as well as adopting the Anglo-American model of corporate governance, public institutions, etc.

This last point is critical because it touches on one of the implicit assumptions of the evolving architecture, and could, in the extreme, touch upon some significant sensitivities. It is the assumption that the Anglo-American brand of market economy, with its array of institutions, is the 'best' and should be adopted by everyone irrespective of local conditions and preferences. One could take issue with such an imperial undertone of 'do it my way or be damned' prescription, which challenges people's freedoms and the sovereignty of nation states.

The politics of it is left to history to resolve.[10] More fundamentally however, such a stance threatens the foundation of the market economy.

An enduring insight from Polanyi (1944) is that markets are sustainable only to the extent that they are embedded in social and political institutions. These institutions serve three major functions critical to the survival of the market economy: they *regulate*, *stabilize*, and *legitimate* market outcomes. Students of sociology and anthropology might educate us that such 'social' and 'political' institutions are specific to particular socio-cultural environments, and they evolve over time. Each society, out of its historical, cultural and financial circumstances, evolves these institutions—the basic requirement being that they perform these three functions. Because countries differ, it also means that differences in economic and institutional circumstances would ensure that regimes that work in one setting might not work in others. Wholesale importation of institutions and regulatory standards from abroad may not work. This 'evolutionary' and 'culture-specific' nature of institutions is completely missed by the models of NGFA being foisted upon developing countries. The self-delusion that to be a good capitalist, everyone has to import the Anglo-American style institutions and politics is a portent threat to an orderly evolution of market economies in the developing countries.

What can be made of the foregoing analysis? The message is simple: the assumption that global growth and equity would be 'best' served by deeper financial integration through open capital account and the quest for a world of *mono-economics* is shown to be founded on shaky theoretical and empirical grounds. On a cost-benefit basis, the model of premature and complete liberalization of the capital account is shown to exacerbate the vulnerability of small open (especially poor) economies to crisis but without any tangible benefits. Over time, this exposure could be growth retarding, as the devastating effects of shocks can be permanent. Furthermore, the other pillars of the evolving NGFA are largely half-truths. There is thus a need for a wider debate because there are some insights waiting to be uncovered regarding how small, poor economies work; the best strategies to integrate them into the global economy; and how to manage the global system for rapid and broadly shared growth.

# 4

## Evaluating the Potential Impacts

Beside the appropriateness or adequacy of the framework underlying the NGFA, the specific proposals in the Architecture could have some significant effects—some positive and some negative—on poor countries and people. Despite the deep conceptual and methodological problems in evaluating the potential impacts of the new architecture, some broad generalizations can be made.[11]

### Potential Impacts on Developing Countries

It is important to stress at the outset that as part of the globalization process, deeper financial integration through the NGFA could provide some benefits for some of the 'mature' economies, but could also ruin the underdeveloped ones and exacerbate the global inequality. The NGFA essentially aims to 'strengthen' an existing system rather than the creation of a new one, and targets mostly the OECD countries and the systemically significant emerging market economies. Thus, for economies that already have the requisite institutions and are already operating on the frontiers of the 'integrated' global financial system, the proposals basically aim to plug some observed loopholes in the system.

In principle, even for the poorest of developing countries, it is difficult to quarrel with a system that leads to greater transparency, accountability, better standards, codes and principles. Since the NGFA does not have in its sight the very poor countries, often with very thin money and capital markets, it does not address the issues pertaining to the 'evolutionary process' for those that do not already have the prerequisites. By 'strengthening' the position of the major players in the global economy without adequate attention to 'pull along' the weakest segment of the global system, the NGFA might, in the end, contribute to deepening global inequality. Indeed, since global capital account liberalization is the goal of the NGFA as part of the efforts to strengthen the globalization process, it may be fair to infer that the broad outcome would be the exacerbation of the current chasm between the rich and the poor countries.

Since the proponents of globalization attribute every good thing in the world to the process, it is also fair to attribute the ensuing inequity to it. As Box 1 illustrates, global inequality has been widening during the period of deeper integration. While a one-to-one mapping of cause and effect relationships is difficult, there are bases to infer that financial integration of asymmetrical economies can lead to massive capital 'flight' from the poorer countries to the richer ones. That is the main point of Williamson (1990) which was noted earlier. Richer economies not only provide greater safety but also higher risk-adjusted rates of return. So far, only about a dozen developing countries have benefited from capital inflows from the richer economies. Others have generally been net capital exporters to the west, when account is taken of the 'capital flight'.

The second issue is that the impact on poor countries would depend on their 'initial conditions'. From the analysis in Chapter III above, it is evident that small economies are highly vulnerable to financial crises and the consequences can be damaging. Whether countries benefit or be damned by deeper financial integration would therefore depend on the extent to which they have succeeded in putting in place appropriate institutions and prerequisites for effective functioning of a market economy. To what extent are institutions for social safety nets (systems of social insurance) developed? To what extent is the domestic financial system developed and effectively linked to the productive sector? Is domestic financial liberalization completed and effective? To what extent are the supply side bottlenecks (transaction costs) eliminated to ensure that financial inflows can be channelled into productive investment? As noted earlier, Wolfensohn observes that inadequate attention to these 'preconditions for a market economy' has caused much of the ruin in Russia. Without relevant structural and institutional development, as well as development of markets for goods and services, openness or financial integration may not produce any tangible benefits (contrast the experiences of Poland and Russia in Box 2 below). In general, the impacts of the NGFA would depend on the location of the particular country on the spectrum of development as a mature market economy. Given the significance of 'initial conditions' on the likely impacts, a potentially useful classification of developing countries would be (i) the systemically significant emerging markets and (ii) all the others. The emerging market countries that have already substantially adopted capital account convertibility include Indonesia, South Korea, Malaysia, Philippines and Thailand in Asia; South Africa; and Argentina, Brazil, Chile, Venezuela and Mexico in Latin America. China and India, although major recipients of foreign private capital flows, have not yet significantly opened up their capital accounts. What are the likely impacts of the NGFA on these emerging markets? Again, it will depend on individual country circumstances.

A salient feature of these economies, which might continue in the future, is that they have been the major recipients of financial flows to developing countries. Net (foreign) private capital inflows to all developing countries averaged at more than $200 billion per year during 1996-1997, while total official capital flows were around $25 billion per year during 1992-1997. (Actually net official capital flows were negative during 1996.) Net foreign direct investment accounted for about two-thirds of the total flows, with net portfolio investment at around 30 percent, and Bank loans and others making up the rest. The bulk of the flows (more than 90 percent) were to the 12 emerging market countries[12] (see Appendix Tables 1 and 2). The impacts of these capital flows on the economies would depend on the composition of the inflows (between short-term and long-term), and the absorptive capacity of the economies. It would also put them at very high risk of future crises and contagion. An important point to note is that many, if not all, of these emerging markets liberalized their capital accounts following the increasing maturity of their institutions and product markets, and not preceding these developments. Furthermore, foreign direct investment (FDI) has been known to flow into large, profitable economies with secure property rights (or small economies that are linked to larger markets), and open capital account is not necessarily the most important determinant of FDI.

## Specific Impacts on Poor Countries

The specific elements of the NGFA could also impact on poor countries adversely. A few of them are examined in the following.

There are elements of the NGFA, which are introduced as insurance mechanisms, but these could have the effects of increasing the cost of borrowing by the poor countries. One element of the NGFA is the requirement for borrowing countries to self-insure against the risks of financial crises, at least partially. Elements of these include enlarged foreign exchange reserve holdings by borrowing countries and increased reserve requirements for borrowing and lending banks. Both entail significant increases in costs of funds to the countries and the institutions. Another recommendation deals with the introduction of clauses in bonds and/or loan agreements with foreign private creditors to facilitate debt workouts including rescheduling based on agreement with a

## Box 1: Globalization and Global Inequality

The world today is divided between those who benefit from globalization and those who lose. The OECD economies and some emerging markets seem to be net beneficiaries. At the other extreme are the many countries benefiting little from expanding markets and advancing technology. Madagascar, Niger, the Russian Federation, Tajikistan and Venezuela are among them.

These countries are becoming even more marginal—ironic, since many of them are highly 'integrated', with exports nearly 30 percent of GDP for Sub-Saharan Africa and only 19 percent for the OECD countries. But these developing countries hang on the vagaries of global markets, with the prices of primary commodities having fallen to their lowest levels in a century and a half. They have shown little growth in exports and attracted virtually no foreign investment. In sum, today, global opportunities are unevenly distributed between countries and people.

If global opportunities are not shared better, the failed growth of the last decades will continue. Today, more than 80 countries still have per capita incomes that are lower than they were a decade or more ago. While 40 countries have sustained average per capita income growth of more than 3 percent a year since 1990, 55 countries, mostly in Sub-Saharan Africa and Eastern Europe and the Commonwealth of Independent States (CIS), have had declining per capita incomes.

Many people are also missing out on employment opportunities. The global labor market is increasingly integrated for the highly skilled—corporate executives, scientists, entertainers and the many others who form the global professional elite—with high mobility and wages. But the market for unskilled labor is highly restricted by national barriers.

Inequality has been rising in many countries since the early 1980s. In China disparities are widening between the export-oriented regions of the coast and the interior: the human poverty index is just under 20 percent in coastal provinces, but more than 50 percent in inland Guizhou.

The countries of Eastern Europe and the CIS have registered some of the largest increases ever in the Gini coefficient, a measure of income inequality. OECD countries also registered big increases in inequality after the 1980s especially Sweden, theUnited Kingdom and the United States.

Inequality between countries has also increased. The income gap between the fifth of the world's people living in the richest countries and the fifth in the poorest was 74 to 1 in 1997, up from 60 to 1 in 1990 and 30 to 1 in 1960. In the 19th century, too, inequality grew rapidly during the last three decades, in an era of rapid global integration: the income gap between the top and bottom countries increased from 3 to 1 in 1820 to 7 to 1 in 1870 and 11 to 1 in 1913.

By the late 1990s the fifth of the world's population living in the highest income countries had: 86 percent of world GDP—the bottom fifth just 1 percent; 82 percent of world export markets—the bottom fifth just 1 percent; 68 percent of foreign direct investment—the bottom fifth just 1 percent; 74 percent of world telephone lines, today's basic means of communication—the bottom fifth just 1.5 percent.

Some pundits have predicted convergence. Yet the past decade has shown increasing concentration of income, resources and wealth among people, corporations and countries. For example, OECD countries, with 19 percent of the global population, have 71 percent of global trade in goods and services, 58 percent of foreign direct investment and 91 percent of all internet users.

The world's 200 richest people more than doubled their net worth in the four years to 1998, to more than $1 trillion. The assets of the top three billionaires are more than the combined GNP of all least developed countries and their 600 million people.

All these trends are not the inevitable consequences of global economic integration—but they run ahead of global governance to share the benefits.

**Source**: UNDP (1999: 2-3).

majority of the creditors. This would also increase the cost of funds from private sources. A third facet relates to defaults by borrowers on interest and/or principal payments on loans from private creditors, with the implicit or explicit blessing of the IMF, and the provisions under the NGFA for the Fund to continue to lend to countries with such arrears. This too might increase the cost of funds to compensate for the increased risk to the private lenders. Recent examples of such defaults include Russia and Ecuador. In fact, the cost of funds might increase not only for the defaulting countries, but also to several other borrowers. Overall, some analysts believe that the cost of borrowing would increase under the emerging NGFA.

Under the NGFA, developing countries, especially those in need of the Fund assistance, would have to brace themselves for much further erosion of their sovereignty.[13] The kind of reform packages designed and foisted by the Fund on Indonesia, South Korea and Thailand as preconditions for its assistance gives insights into the nature of conditionality under the NGFA. For example, as a quid pro quo for the Fund's support, these countries had to sign on to agreements with the Fund that contained between '50 to 80 detailed conditions covering everything from the deregulation of garlic monopolies to taxes on cattle feed and new environmental laws',[14] many issues on which the IMF may have limited understanding and/or expertise. More than ever, the international system is poised to remolding the developing countries that come for financial assistance to conform to the Anglo-American way of life. While it is acceptable for European countries to exist with significant rigidities in their labor market (that produces 12 percent unemployment rate), the Asian countries have been forced to implement the most detailed labor market reforms that have thrown millions out of job. The irony is that the labor market had nothing to do with the crisis. In essence, the message of the NGFA to poor countries is: you haven't seen anything yet in terms of conditionality.

Furthermore, with the proposals for a series of 'common codes' and insistence on activist surveillance by the IMF, development advice and assistance is likely to become obsessed with 'book-keeping' rather than about people and the vulnerable groups. In the evaluation of its adjustment programs, the IMF adopts such indicators as budget deficits, exchange rate premiums, etc., as 'performance criteria' but not unemployment rate, poverty, or other people-oriented indicators. There is the danger that with the NGFA driven largely by the IMF, the 'performance targets' will detract from the well-being of people

## Box 2: Poland Prospers While Russia Deteriorates: Why?

### Poland

In the late 1980s, when Poland embarked on opening its economy, it took a 'shock therapy' approach to macroeconomic management. In the first few years of transition, income and consumption dropped by some 20 percent and unemployment and poverty increased. But in 1994 human development trends started improving and economic growth took off. Consumption increased and unemployment fell from more than 16 percent in 1993 to less than 10 percent in 1997.

What made the difference? Poland shifted in the mid-1990s from a piecemeal to a comprehensive approach. The building blocks of the program were institutional reforms, policy consistency and popular participation.

At the beginning of the transition Poland established a democratic system with market institutions, including property rights and a transparent financial sector. There was a strong political will to advance reforms and a consensus on the transition strategy. Policies aimed at building the market system with a comprehensive approach towards privatization and modernization of the industrial base. This differed from the rushed and uncontrolled privatization in Russia, from the market option in Hungary, and from the equity option in the Czech Republic. By negotiating with banks and other partners, and in some cases undertaking debt swaps, Poland solved the debt problems of the state enterprises.

Openness policies remained consistent despite changes in government, and there was a consensus on opening to the world economy, joining the OECD, European Union and North Atlantic Treaty Organization (NATO), and adopting internal policies related to privatization, economic restructuring and decentralization. All policies balanced market and equity considerations.

And all policies were the subject of public debate in parliament and the media. This gave a sense of transparency and ownership, facilitating consensus. Compare that with Russia, where a narrow group of people made decisions whenever policies were subject to internal conflict.

**Russia**

In 1997 Russia's exports to the rest of the world were $56 billion—and its inflows of foreign direct investment $6 billion, or about 30 percent of the total to the region. But its economic growth was a meager 0.4 percent. During 1989- 96, the Gini coefficient of income distribution in Russia deteriorated from 0.24 to 0.48, a doubling of inequality. Wages fell 48 percent, with the share of wage income down from 74 percent to 55 percent and that of rent and other income up almost fourfold, from 5 percent to 23 percent. There are also serious human deprivations. Between 1989 and 1996 male life expectancy declined by more than four years to 60, two years less than the average for developing countries. The under-five mortality rate is 25 per 1,000 live births, compared with 14 in Poland. Homicides and illegal drug trafficking have increased.

What went wrong? Sometimes Russia's problems are seen as only a financial crisis—partly due to the East Asian crisis, unfavorable external conditions and a lack of progress in building market institutions. A broader view sees deeper causes: an imperfect market economy, bad governance, and no rule of law. The lesson is that in the absence of appropriate institutional and market foundations, financial flows and increased trade cannot provide succor to an embattled economy.

**Source**: Ruminska-Zimny 1999 (UNDP, 1999)

and will be judged in terms of how far countries have implemented the 'codes' and 'standards'.

The financial markets are essentially concerned with the production, processing, dissemination and utilization of information. Generation of increased information under the emerging NGFA is desirable. However, the costs of compiling and disseminating such information in a timely manner should be weighted against the likely benefits. Already, some critics are skeptical about the capacities of the global financial markets (investors) to analyse and interpret the data in a constructive fashion. In fact, they point out that any signs and/or threats of weakening of a major institution or economy of a country may precipitate a crisis due to the actions of the global financial markets based on such information. As a result, the risk/frequency of crises may actually increase under the NGFA.

Furthermore, for the poorest developing countries, the budgetary cost of implementing the myriad of codes and standards can be enormous. For example, Finger and Schuler (1999) show that the cost of implementing just some tiny aspects of the WTO commitments was significant for many developing countries. Thus, poor and heavily aid-dependent economies such as Tanzania had to spend some $10 million on modernizing its customs operation; Madagascar spent $11 million to implement sanitary and phytosanitary standards; Algeria spent $112 million on Locust control; and Russia spent $150 million to improve the disease control component of food processing facilities. These are only the minimal aspects of the spending required to comply with global 'standards'. Imagine then what the total spending would mean for the budgets of these poor countries. For the NGFA, the requirements for data collection and processing, as well as strengthening the regulatory and supervisory standards would, for sure, require technical assistance, equipment, training, and computerization. Without these being funded by external grants, the cash strapped governments would have little choice but to squeeze the budget for most vulnerable groups—social sector programs and protection of the environment. This is because, though the tone of the proposals sounds as if they are optional, in practice they are mandatory since they are preconditions for participation in and borrowing from the international capital market. The implications for and impact on public expenditure, provision of public goods, social infrastructure and services are worrisome. Past experience with IMF's SAPs bear out this concern.

Within countries, how the NGFA impacts on different groups would depend on existing asset and income distribution, the impact of NGFA on growth and budgetary allocation, as well as the prevailing conditions before the reforms. One of the pillars of the NGFA is domestic financial liberalization. According to Stewart (1998:8), 'the impact of liberalization on income distribution and poverty depends on what the liberalization is *from*. If the prior situation is the stereotypical one, of an elite gaining privileged access to most resources (e.g. credit, employment and foreign exchange) then a market solution would be likely to extend access to the poor compared with the prior situation. But if in the previous situation state benefits did succeed in reaching the poor (e.g. through employment schemes, credit allocation, and food subsidies) then the more market oriented solution may well deprive some of the poor of resources'. In many developing countries, the situation has been mixed although financial liberalization under SAPs has eliminated most of the controlled regimes. It is not certain that the NGFA would go much further than existing programs.

But generally, financial liberalization may, at least in the short- and medium-runs, help those with assets more. Reform of the domestic financial systems of the developing countries including the banking sector and other financial intermediaries may have unexpected adverse short-term impacts on the low-income people and small businesses. Kenya presents an interesting example of the potential impacts of banking sector reforms on the poor. Recently, Kenya opened its banking system and allowed foreign banks to compete with local banks. In early 1999, the Central Bank allowed the banks to set the minimum balances to be maintained by customers in their savings and checking accounts. The foreign banks promptly increased the minimum balances from between Ksh.1,000 to Ksh.2,500 to Ksh.5,000 to Ksh.10,000. As a result, many low-income clients could not afford to continue to obtain retail-banking services from the foreign banks. At the same time, the financial health and viability of domestic banks became a serious concern with a few weak banks kicked out of the clearance system and closed. The safety of client money in other domestic banks was also at risk. The citizens who could not afford to bank with the foreign banks had no choice but to choose between the risky domestic banks or keep their meagre funds under their pillows. The latter option was also risky in a milieu of increasing robberies and crime.

Furthermore, for many poor developing countries, the adoption of strict market/profit criteria by the banks may result in branch consolidation and reduction in access to banking services. These effects may be most severe in rural areas, for low-income/poor consumers (savers and borrowers) and small businesses. The minimal social programs hitherto implemented by the banks may be jeopardized. Indeed, the emphasis on purely market-mediated solutions could deny many developing countries with weak or missing markets the opportunity to strategically engineer the development of certain sectors of the economy through directed credit. Small farmers often benefit from fertilizer subsidies and directed credit. Given the predominance of women in small-scale farming, the removal of such credit and subsidies might affect women's productivity and further drive them down the poverty trench.

An element of the NGFA (at least as defined by Rubin) is 'adhering to core labor standards'. This same issue has been raised at the WTO negotiations and it was agreed in 1996 to leave labor matters to the International Labor

Organization. Having failed to enforce it at the WTO, it is unclear why labor standard should now be smuggled in as part of the global financial architecture. Beside the fact that the enforcement of these standards—whatever they may mean—would be very harmful to developing countries' competitiveness, especially the poorest ones. There are a number of other reasons for objecting to them. As the London *Financial Times* (October 13, 1999:26) states the argument for such standards is very weak. According to the *Times*,

> Much of the argument turns on the dubious claim that low labor standards amount to unfair competition. But the most common explanation of appalling working conditions is extreme poverty, not mercantilism. Poor countries generate a tiny fraction of world exports, while the World Bank estimates that less than 5 per cent of their child labor is employed in export industries... Western governments know this. So why are they renewing their demands...? Most admit in private that they lack a persuasive intellectual case....

The point here is that the key reason for understanding issues of 'poor' labor standards is poverty. In a country with 70 per cent of the population living in absolute poverty, it is difficult to see what kind of social insurance or labor 'standards' can be implemented. For illustration, consider a widow in a poor African country with five children (the husband having died of AIDS). Per capita annual income is $100, and in such an environment, there can't be a reasonable social insurance such as 'welfare checks' and 'food stamps' and the widow cannot afford to send them to school. The family cannot find adequate food to eat let alone think about education. A dilemma emerges. Should the widow moralize about having the 12 and 14 year olds work in the cocoa farms (exportable sector) and risk the family starving to death or violate the 'international labor standards' and be alive? In other words, it is important to underscore the point that most of the issues about 'standards' have to do with the nature of underdevelopment, and hence the 'lack of standards' need to be understood in many cases to be symptoms rather than causes of underdevelopment. Without addressing the underlying causes—most important of which is poverty—coercing poor countries to enforce certain labor standards amounts to punishing the victims.

There is another objection to this quest for 'harmonization' at all levels. It is not only impractical but largely indefensible. Competitive advantages are largely about differences in natural endowments, regulations, institutions, transaction costs, and even social and cultural norms. International exchange is warranted basically because of these differences. Labor is certainly one key factor of production, and its costs and productivity confer competitive advantage on countries and firms within them. It is certainly up to countries and their governments, given their preferences and capacity, to decide what kinds of regulations, institutions, and business practices would help it compete in the global system. Lower cost environments with high productivity of labor would attract investments from the rest of the world. It is ironic that the western countries only look at the areas where they seem to lose competitive advantages—labor and environmental issues.

Consider an argument by the poorer countries that some of the reasons why they are not competitive are because of the huge brain drain as well as massive capital flight from their economies to the west. The western countries, because of their higher development, offer higher wages to labor, and greater returns to capital. Would it be fair then for poorer countries to demand, as part of the levelling of the playing field, for the western countries to lower their wages (so as not to attract away the scarce skilled labor from poorer countries) or to refuse savings from poor countries? Some analysts in the developing countries point to the selective nature of the imposition of these international standards. They find it surprising that the western countries, which have asserted competitive advantage (or complete monopoly), of the high-technology industries also, wish to eliminate the only competitive advantage of poorer countries—cheap labor.

Finally, it is important to commend the 'promise' under the NGFA to protect social spending at pre-crisis levels in countries that suffer from crisis in the future. This is an important recognition, but the problem is that such concerns are designed as emergency measures during crises and not as systematic programs to eliminate human and material poverty. The challenge is to design an architecture that systematically integrates social issues and poverty eradication as the central objective.

# 5

## Towards an Inclusive Architecture

### People, Poverty and the NGFA

There is a global consensus that at the end of the Twentieth century, the single most important development challenge is the endemic and pervasive poverty, which has engulfed more than two-thirds of humanity, despite the rapid globalization of trade and finance. Given its dimensions, poverty therefore poses the most portent systemic risk to the national and global economies. Not surprisingly, development programming of any kind is increasingly about mainstreaming the agenda of poverty reduction. Unfortunately, even if fully implemented, the current NGFA misses this point with its obsession with macro-financial statistics. Systematic linkages to the human development concerns are sorely missing, and the victims might be the more than four billion low-income and poor people.

### Some Elements of an Inclusive NGFA

The fundamental objective that must underlie a people-oriented, socially inclusive architecture should be to reconcile the demands of efficiency with equity, thereby taming and harnessing global finance to serve people. This requires a high level of creativity but unfortunately there is acute shortage of ideas in this regard. It would be foolhardy to offer a template but suffice it to suggest that such a socially inclusive NGFA would require actions in at least three levels: (i) bringing back, and re-defining the role of, the state in the NGFA; (ii) programs to reconcile the imperatives of the social agenda as defined at the World Summit for Social Development with the interests of the main actors in the global financial markets; and (iii) participation of the poor countries in defining the global agenda. The participation of these countries would also empower them to bring to the table some of their priority concerns which are currently swept under the rug (e.g. elimination of the multiple standards in the definition and implementation of accountability and transparency, designing adequate safeguards for differential and special treatments, and a global lending system that avoids the moral hazard problems of the lenders' behaviour). These issues are elaborated upon briefly in the following:

The first key element in designing a socially inclusive NGFA is to bring back the state, not only in supervision and prudential oversight of the financial system, but also to manage financial flows and allocation to achieve equitable growth. Strictly market-based solutions—especially in the context of weak or missing markets, institutions, imperfect or asymmetric information, 'animal spirits', and contagion—are hardly the best means to guarantee financial stability, growth and equity.

The lessons of history are emphatic on this. According to Stiglitz (1998b:7), three major lessons of history regarding the role of the state in the development of capitalist societies, but which are often ignored by mainstream economists in their thinking on globalization and the NGFA are that: (i) 'successful development efforts in the United States as well as many other countries had involved a very active role for government; (ii) many societies in decades before active government involvement—or interference, as these doctrines would put it—failed to develop; indeed, development was the exception around the world, not the rule; and (iii) worse still, capitalist economies before the era of greater government involvement were characterized not only by high levels of economic instability, but also by widespread social/economic problems; large groups, such as the aged and the unskilled, were often left out of any progress and were left destitute in the economic crashes that occurred with such regularity'.

The NGFA should therefore be designed in terms of useful benchmarks and 'minimum' standards, and leave sufficient room for the governments to manoeuvre. The role to be played by a government should depend on the country circumstances, the capacity of the government, and the stage of development of its institutions and markets. Since the world is not likely to have a global federal government any time soon, national governments must still be relied upon to do whatever they can to maximize the welfare of their citizens, especially where such actions are not likely to jeopardize the welfare of citizens of other countries.

### Reconciling Wall Street with Copenhagen (or Main Street)

With the state firmly in-charge at the national level, the international community faces a major challenge of how to systematically integrate the social objectives into the NGFA. From the review in earlier Chapters, it is evident that the social issues are brought in as useful tack-ons. The interests of the financial moguls in Wall Street and Broad Street seem to dominate in the hope that the presumed benefits would 'trickle down' to the poor. This is an untenable logic, and Wolfensohn may have realized this when he made the statement quoted at the beginning of this monograph. At the World Social Summit in Copenhagen in 1995, the international community set quantitative and time-bound goals and targets for social development in all countries (see Annex 2). The first target date of 2000 is around the corner and it is fair to say that none of the goals and targets will be met. Also, the OECD-DAC augmented the Social Summit, and moved the first target date a bit further away from 2000 (see Annex 3). But meeting even these targets too is in danger. As a part of the Social Summit agreements, developing and developed countries committed to allocate, on average, 20 percent of official development assistance (ODA) and 20 percent of the national budgets, respectively, to basic social programs. It is doubtful that these proposals are being met or are deep enough to make a difference.

Related to the above is the issue of paucity of resources relative to need. For example, the Global Action Plan estimates that it would require about $8 billion annually for ten years to implement programs that would help provide universal access to primary education. Sub-Saharan Africa (SSA) is expected to be the only region that would experience an increase in the number of children out of school in the next decade. Thus, by 2005, SSA will account for half of the estimated 96 million children that will not have access to primary school; by 2015 the region will account for three-quarters of the global total. To remedy this, it is estimated that SSA would require some $3.6 billion per annum to finance the transition to high-quality universal education over a ten-year period. This is for primary education alone. Even with the improved revenue collection efforts by governments, mobilization of the required resources is far beyond the financing capacity of the region. This is all the more alarming in the context of the ever-declining ODA.

So far, evidence indicates that the approaches to the social goals have been ad-hoc and often too little, and the impacts have been minuscule. A major surprise is that even the IMF now agrees with this assessment. After decades of insisting that macroeconomic adjustment was reducing poverty and that globalization was working for all, the IMF has finally come to terms with reality and now argues that: globalization has not benefited the poor; poverty is increasing not reducing; and while macro stabilisation is necessary for growth and poverty reduction, the causation also runs the other way such that without effective poverty reduction, macro stabilisation and growth will not be sustainable (see Box 3).

What does this specifically mean for the IMF? For many years, IMF-supported programs have explicitly incorporated social considerations but the interrelationship between growth and social development now needs to be more precisely defined.

The ideas presented in Box 3 above represent a major intellectual shift on the part of the IMF. It is important to consolidate and improve upon this momentum for change. Combining the poverty reduction and growth facility with the 'enhanced' HIPC initiative can make some difference in providing additional resources to the embattled heavily indebted poor countries. However, relative to need—the magnitude of poverty and the budgetary outlays required to make a dent on it—one is not sure about the size of impact of the new initiatives. For example, the ECA (1999) estimates that it might take annual inflows of ODA of no less than 15 percent of Africa's GDP for a decade to make a dent on poverty. Judged against this requirement, it is not clear how far the new IMF facility can go. While the IMF recognizes that a new, bold initiative is required as a collaborative effort at the global level, its proposals seem to be somewhat of an anti-climax merely tinkering at the margins. The size of the resources for the new Poverty Reduction and Growth Facility is not known, and more so, the conditionality that would go with lending from the Facility. These are issues that call for greater transparency and debate. Sometimes, the conditionalities attached to the Fund lending can obviate the potential benefits to the recipient countries.

Ultimately, the challenge of global poverty needs bold, radical moves. Currently, the globalization process is deepening but without a governance structure that manages the inequities that go with it. There is no mandatory transfer mechanisms (such as the social insurance systems in the OECD countries) to cater to the needs of those squeezed out of global competition. Development assistance depends largely on the goodwill and altruism of the rich countries and rich people. However, the generosity of the rich countries as measured by the ratio of official development assistance (ODA) to GDP has been on the decline for several years and is at less than half of the target of 0.7 percent agreed to more than 20 years ago. In an earlier paper, Soludo (1999) had called for a globalization tax as one means of making such a transfer mandatory. But in the absence of a global 'federal government', such a tax might be a distant proposal. The absence of a global government should not however stop the world from creatively thinking about non-market solutions to reconcile the demands of competitive finance with equity. Deep debt relief or forgiveness conditional on the respective countries spending the potential released service payments on social programs could be one way to go. Besides that, what is wrong with using the proceeds of a 'Global Tobin Tax' to make transfers to the 50 poorest countries to fund social programs? Other avenues such as the institution of capital gains taxes within countries could be used to finance a number of social programs. The point is that there is room for creative thinking and action beyond minute incrementalism that seem to characterize the current initiatives.

## Participation: Whose Architecture?

So far, a 'global' financial architecture is being designed by less than 10 percent of countries. Within the OECD, and the various groups such as G-22, G-33 and G-21, there are complaints that the process was being rammed down by the G-7 countries. Even within the G-7, the de facto power is the U.S. Treasury. Rodrik (1999c) captures this concentration of decision making when he notes in respect of the evolving architecture that 'ideas coming out of Europe principally from Britain and France have been more ambitious, but they are not likely to get far without U.S. backing'. Not to miss the point about who is in charge of the architecture, Rubin assured the House of Representatives Committee on Banking and Financial Services (on May 20, 1999) that 'Overall, the aim of President Clinton's approach is to build an international financial system...'. He went on to 'focus on some of the most important elements of our work...'. It turns out that 'President Clinton's approach' is actually 'the' new architecture. So much for formulation of a participatory or democratic global governance system! The imperial manner of the design, approval and on-going implementation raises serious questions about the legitimacy of the NGFA.

Furthermore, there are questions about how the concerns and aspirations of the poor developing countries can be heard, taken into consideration, and incorporated in the design of the NGFA. According to Griffith-Jones, *et al.* (1999:65), 'Much emphasis has also been placed on the development of numerous standards, and their implementation by developing countries. A source of concern is that developing countries—especially low-income ones—do not

**41**

on the whole participate much in the definition of those standards, though they are being asked to implement them'. Probably the assumption could be that these low-income countries do not have anything to contribute to the NGFA or that what is good for Wall Street should be good for the poor countries and their people as well.[15] Neither of these assumptions reflects the critical development lessons of the final quarter of the Twentieth Century.

## Some Issues Relevant to Poor Countries

Were developing countries allowed to participate in the process, they would have had a chance to voice their concerns regarding the appropriateness or adequacy of the provisions of the NGFA for their local conditions. They would have been able to articulate their demand for a program of bailing in, since they are not likely (in the near future) to have the crises requiring a bailout; demand for a truly transparent global financial system; argue for an insurance against the moral hazard posed by the lending practices of donors; etc. Brief elaborations on a few of these missing items are included in the following, which would have given the developing countries some sense of inclusion.

### Poor Countries Need Bailing In, Not Bailing Out

Beside the systemically significant emerging markets, there are more than 100 other developing countries with a few billion people whose economies have rudimentary financial institutions and are almost completely by-passed by the developments in the global system. In most of these economies, more than 50 percent of production takes place in the informal sector. More than 60 percent of their population lives on less that $1 a day. In these environments, the issues are about the nuts and bolts of daily subsistence, and a fundamental challenge is how to 'create' and 'promote' the development of a formal and viable financial system that can be used as a potent vehicle for poverty eradication. Thus, for most of these economies, there is not likely a financial crisis waiting for a bailout package. What they might need is a package to help them 'build' viable financial systems. These economies are experiencing the worst form of financial crisis, albeit in a subtle form—capital flight—thereby perpetuating their destitution. A reversal of this trend remains a fundamental challenge to the NGFA.

Caprio (1999) summarizes the state of the financial systems in the poor developing countries. Among the 160 countries for which data was compiled, the total assets of the financial systems of the poorest 52 countries with 200 million people were less than the assets of the World Bank-IMF Staff Credit Union. The assets of the financial systems in the bottom half (80) of the 160 developing countries with 500 million people were less than those of one of the smallest savings and loan institutions in Frederick (Maryland), a suburb of Washington, D.C. It is therefore not surprising that these economies are not active participants in the global financial markets. For example, the flow of net private capital to Sub-Saharan Africa averaged at a mere 5 percent of the total flows to all developing countries, with the bulk (almost two-thirds) of these flows directed to South Africa. The experience of Africa's integration into the global financial system and the prospects are illustrated in Box 4.

So, what can be done to help these economies build viable financial systems and less risky environments for FDI? According to Caprio (1999), a number of extraordinary measures may be needed to build a safe and sound banking system in a very small economy. He suggests alternative approaches such as allowing good foreign banks to operate in the country or for the country to become a partner in a regional banking system (such as the CFA Franc zone in West Africa?) to speed up the process of integration into the global system. These are useful suggestions.

However, the proposals by Caprio assume that the problem is merely that of size. But the size of these financial systems might be connected with other structural bottlenecks. Two factors come to mind: risk and transaction costs, which themselves are linked to security, debt overhang, and infrastructural decay. In today's world, most of the 52 poorest countries are either in conflicts or emerging from them. There is a high level of correlation between poverty and armed conflict. Conflicts deter savings-investment and cause 'capital flight'. Capital flight is another form of financial crisis, but because it often does not happen with a big bang, or is less noticed in the major world economies, the issue is completely missing from the current discussions on the NGFA. How do we make all places on earth safe for profitable investment, given that population migration is not yet an element of 'globalization'? Can the world muster the will to implement a Twenty-first Century Marshall Plan to build the human and physical infrastructural bases for the poorest countries of Africa and elsewhere so that FDI can find it profitable to locate there?

The domestic savings rate in many of these poor countries is a mere 15 percent. With 40 percent of the population living in absolute poverty, little can be expected in terms of increased savings from a population that is barely able

**43**

**Box 3: IMF Rediscovers Its Mission and Reforms Itself into a Development Institution**

The IMF Managing Director, Michel Camdessus (1999b) has rediscovered the central mission of the Fund as stated in Article 1: "to facilitate the expansion and balanced growth of international trade, and to contribute thereby to the *promotion and maintenance of high levels of employment and real income and to the development of the productive resources of all members as primary objectives of economic policy*". Camdessus admits that previous approaches to realizing this objective have not worked. Consequently, poverty has intensified, and new approaches are called for. In his recent speeches, Camdessus propounds on some of the issues as follows:

**Globalization and Poverty**

"...globalization is not necessarily a bad thing, but something that has the potential for improving living standards around the world.... The poor have not benefited and the world's response is still not up to the fundamental challenge of harmonizing globalization. To my mind, the most pressing global issue that faces us as we approach the end of the century is poverty: four billion people (two-thirds of humanity) are living in unacceptable conditions that are scarcely better than when the century began. In conference after conference, we—advanced countries and developing and transition economies—have made pledges to promote development for the benefit of the very poor. Central among the seven pledges is one—from the Copenhagen Declaration—to reduce by one-half the level of extreme poverty by the year 2015. This, and all the other goals, will not be achieved through piecemeal measures, but through comprehensive collaborative action. To our mind, *the fight against poverty is an essential component of the reform of the international monetary and financial architecture*" (emphasis added).

**New Compacts, New Orientation**

"... Let me recall the values behind this effort, the values that seek to humanize a world in search of unity, the values in which people can find common ground. Three are closely interrelated: responsibility, solidarity, and citizenship. Responsibility because now more than ever every country, no matter what its size, is responsible not only for its own destiny but for that of the other countries of the world; solidarity because it is clear that we will not make progress in reducing poverty without a large-scale effort of international solidarity; and citizenship because it is urgent that we broaden our citizenship to cover the new dimensions of problems that have become global problems".

**Framework for the New Approach**

From its experience as a monetary institution, the IMF has learned much about the connections among sound monetary and economic policies, high quality growth, and poverty reduction. This experience may be summarized in the following propositions: One, it is now solidly demonstrated that price stability, fiscal discipline and structural reform promote economic growth; Two, economic growth is a sine qua non and the most significant single factor that contributes to poverty reduction; Three, there is increasing evidence that lower inflation also enhances income equality. In other words, yes, macroeconomic adjustment ultimately benefits the poor. And structural policies also: dismantling product and factor market rigidities helps reduce poverty by increasing not only the supply of essential goods but also the poor's access to them... But now it is also much better understood that the effect also runs in the other direction. The relation here is not linear but circular. To maintain the discipline of strong economic and financial policy long enough to eradicate inflation and to contribute to sustainable growth, it must be implemented in a context in which integral parts of government policies include the fight against poverty, the adoption of appropriate social safety nets, and a recognizable effort to reduce severe inequalities in income distribution over time. This point is essential as far as I am concerned and we must see to it that it is universally understood... In a word, it is clear that sustained poverty reduction will not be achieved without sound macroeconomic policy. But equally, sound economic policies cannot be sustained if 'patent inequity' is left unaddressed.... Following an in-depth analysis of our experience thus far we reached agreement at our Annual Meetings last month to resolutely elevate the fight against poverty to center-stage in IMF's programs for the poorest countries.

**New Instruments?**

Social and economic policies go hand in hand. This is evident in a new strategy for the poorest countries—78 in all—including the 41 most heavily indebted, which emphasizes:

- Taking advantage of the readiness of key creditor countries to expand debt reduction for the heavily indebted poor countries (HIPCs) so as to encourage and help them to allocate the resources thus freed up to poverty reduction and human development;

- Organizing much closer cooperation in this domain between the two Bretton Woods institutions so that we may more effectively serve the heavily indebted poor countries. As you know, of the two institutions, it is the Bank, not the Fund that has developed the expertise to help countries develop their social policies. The poverty reduction strategies that will be a central feature of our new facility will allow coordinated input from international agencies—the World Bank, the United Nations, other donors—and civil society in the interested countries to assist governments in implementing the broad social objectives, while allowing the IMF to stay in the domain of macroeconomic policy and its coordination with social priorities; and

- To this end—this is the third component—establishing a new, highly concessional lending instrument whose name describes its purpose: the Poverty Reduction and Growth Facility (PRGF).

to subsist. But even this meagre saving is sent abroad. Current estimates show that Africa's GDP needs to grow by at least 7 percent per annum in order to reduce poverty by half by the year 2015. To achieve this, it is estimated that an investment rate of 33 percent of GDP would be needed. With a 15 percent saving rate, this leaves a financing gap of 18 percent of GDP to be met from external sources. With ODA at 9 percent and falling, the gap is huge. This regional average masks the wide sub-regional differences: North Africa has a financing gap of just 2 percent, while the Central African region needs some 27 percent of the GDP.

The consequence of the serious shortfalls in investable resources is that the expected growth and development would not happen. Poverty would deepen, and socio-political instability and civil strife would intensify. Capital flight would continue and FDI would be deterred. With a heavy debt burden, a high debt service obligation and dwindling ODA, Africa's brand of financial integration would be a means to channel the meagre savings of the poor Continent to Wall Street and Broad Street.

Furthermore, modern financial transactions are driven mainly by 'sentiments', 'confidence', and 'fundamentals'. How would investors interpret fundamentals or build confidence, in an economy with an external debt stock the size of its GDP, and that is dependent on new borrowings (in domestic and overseas markets) to service its existing debt? Even for FDI, such perverse 'fundamental' as external debt overhang is deterring, as the debt signals the potential of future increases in taxes. It is difficult to imagine that productive capital (FDI) would surge into such an environment. Now that the initial HIPC initiative for debt relief has been shown to be grossly inadequate and the enhanced initiative only somewhat better in resolving the debt burden, can more adequate and bolder initiatives be accommodated within the NGFA?

## Developing Countries Need a Truly 'Transparent' Global System

Transparency and accountability are the new buzzwords of the international development discourse. It is important that these words are defined and systematically applied in very broad terms. Currently, the definition and application are saddled with multiple standards. Take the example of the massive outflow of 'corruption money' from the poorest developing countries to the rich ones. On the one hand, the world is witnessing the most intrusive incursions into private businesses of countries and individuals in the name of conditionality, codes and standards of transparency and accountability, fight against corruption, etc. However, once these rules are flouted and the 'corruption money' makes it safely to the Western countries, then laws of secrecy and protection of privacy begin to apply.

If this practice is not reversed, indeed if the NGFA fails to institute a global transparency that also ensures personal accountability of sources of deposits and wealth, the global financial architecture would perpetuate corruption and lack of accountability at the national levels of very poor countries. Furthermore, it would enhance the inequality in the global economy with the meagre resources of the poverty-stricken countries siphoned off to buoy the economies of the richer countries. What an irony: those who have more shall be given more, and even the little the poor have shall be taken away and given to those who have. The case of Nigeria presented in Box 5 is very insightful in this regard.

But is Nigeria broke? No. It has been reported in the Nigerian media that within the last two decades, the monies looted from the treasury by some of the ex-military generals and their cronies amounted to more than $100 billion. This is about four times the stock of external debt, and three times the size of Nigeria's GDP. Note that this is just the loot of *a few*, and these monies are in banks located in the U.K, Switzerland, USA, and Germany. Without speculating on what the total loot by all the powerful might be, it would be useful to concentrate on the amount that is verified and known. Imagine what a difference this could make to the economy if the global financial architecture is designed in a way that the rules permit the defrauded citizens of Nigeria to get back their monies. In one swoop, Nigeria could write a check for the $28 billion it owes its external creditors. Imagine that the remaining amount is put in a trust fund and international investment experts hired to invest and manage the funds. Even at a conservative annual return of 15 percent, Nigeria would earn about $13 billion annually. This is more than the total export earnings and amounts to some 30 percent of the GDP. Imagine also that this amount is invested to finance education, health, R&D, infrastructure, institution building, etc. With a democracy that ensures a judicious use of the resources, there is no limit to the growth and development potentials of the country. For sure, Nigeria will be able to surpass all the international targets for social development. More fundamentally, more than 50 million Nigerians can be lifted out of absolute poverty in the next decade. As can be expected, many developing countries are in a situation that is similar to that of Nigeria.

Nigeria is making efforts to recover the loot. But will it succeed? Would the principles of 'transparency, accountability, and fight against corruption' under the NGFA ensure that depositors have to declare the sources of certain large deposits? Currently, cash deposits or withdrawals of $10,000 or more attract some security attention in the US. Money laundering is outlawed. But it depicts multiple standards for the global system: to watch out for the street drug dealer who deposits $12,000 but turn a blind eye when a dictator steals from the helpless citizens and deposits $5 billion. Can the world design an architecture that not only makes money-plundering illegal but also unsafe anywhere in the global financial system? More urgently, can the new architecture design effective 'rules of origin' for deposits, and ensure that looted monies are returned to their true owners?

## *Institutions to Minimize Moral Hazard of Lenders' Behaviour*

This requires re-designing Aid and International Lending Operations to avoid the moral hazard problem. Indeed, the world needs to understand the logic and nature of the moral hazard implicit in any program that requires the most heavily indebted poor countries to repay the multilateral, bilateral, and private debt. To do so would be rewarding the irresponsible behaviour of the lenders, who knew the loans they were giving were either not producing tangible benefits or were being siphoned off by unscrupulous people into private bank accounts, but nevertheless continued to push more loans to these countries. Lenders, especially the World Bank, have been known for 'loan-pushing' or loan 'approval culture': managers are rewarded by the volume of loans they make rather than the productivity and impact of the loans. The fact is that these loans did not generate the benefits, which they were supposed to. Otherwise most of the poor borrowing countries would not be in the kind of distress they are in. The new architecture should ensure risk sharing between lenders and borrowers.

Also, a global bankruptcy institution needs to be erected for sovereign debt. This aspect may require a full project on its own. A new mechanism for international lending especially sovereign debt should be designed. What conditions have to be fulfilled for a debt contract to become a legitimate obligation of the (citizens of a) debtor country? What risks should the official and private lenders be required to bear like in every other banking/lending transaction? How do poor countries sue for, and be given appropriate compensation, as a result of any damages resulting from wrong policy advice especially those leveraged through conditionality piggy-backed to the loans?[16] These are legitimate issues that should be adequately addressed in the NGFA.

## *Safeguards and Provisions for Differential Treatment*

Is there any special provision, such as under the WTO that caters for the needs of those specially disadvantaged and which might be harmed by enforcing the rules for developed economies on the poor and vulnerable ones? Should there be specific provision for graduated capital account liberalization and trade liberalization? This is a sore point. Elbadawi and Helleiner (1998:27) note that

## Box 4: Africa and Global Financial Integration

Currently, portfolio inflows into sub-Saharan Africa are minuscule and concentrated mostly in middle income countries such as South Africa. In some other countries, the minuscule inflows are mostly in response to the artificially high real interest rates on government bonds, which arise because governments are constrained by adjustment programs to resort to the weak money markets for financing budget deficits, caused at least in part by the heavy burden of servicing external debt. FDI is also the lowest in the world (about 5 percent of all flows to the developing countries) and mostly concentrated in the extractive, mining sectors. Thus, resource inflows are largely in the form of ODA with Africa ac counting for the largest recipient of ODA per capita in the last decade. But capital outflows from Africa are immense in the form of debt service payments, capital flight through legitimate channels, and plundering of the treasuries by corrupt leaders. Some analysts have estimated that by the end of the 1980s, African private agents have chosen to hold about 40 percent of their wealth (excluding land) abroad. This speaks volumes about the magnitude of capital flight from the region. Capital flight alone amounted to about $220 billion in the decade of the 1980s, and this figure compares favorably with the total external debt stock of the region. It is not clear that these estimates include money plundered by corrupt leaders and deposited in secret bank accounts in some western countries. For example, recent figures published for Nigeria indicate that the total amount of 'corruption money' plundered by individuals and deposited in the West (e.g. U.K, U.S.A., Switzerland and Germany) amounted to over $100 billion. This situation, to varying degrees, is also true in several other developing countries. The world knows where these monies are and how the owners have acquired them. If these monies were returned to their rightful owners, i.e. the citizens of these countries, the external debt stock of the countries could easily be written-off, with substantial surpluses left over to invest in education, health, and infrastructure. Can the new architecture, especially the clauses regarding 'transparency, accountability, and fight against corruption' address these issues which are critical for the poor countries?

The global financial system poses a real dilemma for Africa. It needs to be integrated, but what it gets by way of inflows is nowhere near what it loses in outflows. The major reason for capital flight and lack of FDI is the riskiness of the investment climate. Africa is thus caught in a vicious circle. Because of lack of resources and debt burden, it cannot afford the kind of massive investments in the people, physical infrastructure, and institutions to make its economic environment less risky. At the same time, capital flight continues, and the region gets poorer and poorer.

Exports from the region are not likely to boom anytime soon. The African farmers, with their primitive hoes and machetes, facing the hostile farming conditions, and with inadequate irrigation, infrastructure and support services, have to compete with farmers in the Western world (under liberalization) whose advantages include not only modern technologies, services and markets but also government subsidies (e.g. the combined OECD farm subsidies in 1998 were about equal to Africa's total GDP).

forcing the 'one-size-fits-all' architecture might be harmful and should be resisted.

Stronger WTO members should refrain from making unreasonable demands upon its weaker ones. The WTO system is still sufficiently weak (and flexible) that, provided that its more powerful members show reasonable restraint, African governments probably have little to fear from an overeager WTO Secretariat. On the historical record, they may have more reason for concern about premature and ideologically-driven pressures toward trade and capital account liberalization from the international financial institutions than from the WTO. Aggressive application of IMF and World Bank conditionality to 'enforce' WTO or IMF (or eventually MAI– Multilateral Agreement on Investment) disciplines upon developing countries is a real potential hazard in the emerging world trade and financial regime, and it will have to be resisted.

It is little surprise that the issue of the speed and sequencing of capital account liberalization is still one of the most controversial aspects of the NGFA. It is important that the IMF has finally come to recognize this point. As Camdessus (1999a:5) states: 'Already most agree with two basic ideas: that liberal capital movements are beneficial to worldwide growth; and that liberalization should follow an orderly path, tailored to each country's situation.

**51**

In the coming months, the IMF will be considering proposals for a gradual, country-specific approach that explicitly recognizes the great variety of country situations'. While the first claim about the benefits of liberal capital account is arguable, the second point about country-specific approaches represents the consensus among many experts. The difficulty is not in recognizing this basic issue but in designing details of how country specific approaches should proceed.

## Conclusions

The central message of this monograph is that the proposals for sound standards and effective prudential oversight are, at best, necessary but not sufficient for a healthy and stable global financial system.[17] The claim of the NGFA to be the 'best' system to promote broadly shared global growth is not supported by either theory or empirical evidence. If anything, the underlying framework of the NGFA which seeks to promote liberal capital movements as an objective can even have the effect of aggravating the inherent instability of the financial system, with long lasting damages to the economies of the poor, vulnerable economies. While it is not certain that the kind of 'standards' and 'codes' being foisted upon the poor countries are appropriate for their circumstances, enforcing these standards would have severe budgetary consequences. At best, the international system might be willing to 'lend' further money to help them implement these largely alien standards, thereby worsening their debt burden. Even more threatening to the competitiveness of the poor countries is the odious attempt to force 'labor standards' into the 'global financial architecture'.

In spite of the potential deleterious impacts of the NGFA on the poor countries, their more than four billion people are completely excluded from the processes and discussions surrounding the formulation of the architecture. They are now required to start implementation. Many of the issues of interest to them are not on the table, with poverty issues brought in as ad-hoc tack-ons. The latter efforts appear to be inadequate and too mechanical to make significant impacts. There is a serious question about the legitimacy of the entire NGFA as a 'global' initiative.

In the very long run (perhaps a few decades in the future), there might be political support for a stronger global governance structure (world federal government, lender-of-last resort). Such an institution would be better equipped to address the many inequities resulting from the globalization process. In the interim, national governments must be empowered under the NGFA to take

## Box 5: Nigeria's Predicament

Nigeria does not need debt forgiveness, but a principled global financial system whose rules are applied uniformly to all.

Nigeria's story not only points to the tragedy of its self-inflicted poverty but also highlights the multiple standards, albeit hypocrisy, of the global financial system. Africa's largest oil producer and its most populous country, Nigeria, used to be also the region's largest economy with a GDP of more than $100 billion and a per capita income of $1150 in 1981. No thanks to two decades of pernicious military misrule, GDP declined to around $38 billion and per capita income to a mere $250 by 1998 in spite of its status as the world's eighth largest oil producer. If there is any country in Africa that has reason not to be in debt, it is Nigeria.

But no. Nigeria's external debt is about $28 billion, amounting to some 300 percent of export receipts. With gyrations in oil prices, its major export, the country has difficulty servicing its debt. As one of the 20 poorest countries (on per capita income basis), Nigeria could very well qualify for the HIPC debt relief. The nearly 120 million Nigerians are bewildered. They have seen their country, the once proud 'giant of Africa', become a dwarf. Some 60 percent of Nigerians now live in absolute poverty, and Nigeria's based on the UNDP's human development index has fallen from 46th among developing countries in 1981 to 146th in 1999. In comparison to Indonesia, a country with very similar initial conditions/characteristics, the tragic decline of Nigeria becomes indefensible.

Finally, after a titanic struggle, the country has now made a successful transition to democracy. But the flagging democracy, with the promise of a new beginning, is hamstrung by the enormity of its socio-economic problems. There are no resources to pay reasonable wages, to rehabilitate schools and hospitals, to service debt, to provide basic infrastructure, etc. As one of the programs to reverse the decay in human development, the government has proposed free and compulsory education up to the 9th grade. All the promises and programs to get the 'giant of Africa' back to its feet and lead the continent in the next millennium will come to naught in the face of serious resource constraints.

charge: take decisive steps, not only to ensure effective supervision and prudential oversight, but more so to tame and harness finance to serve the socio-economic development of their citizens. Without this effective national state intervention, market economy or global finance, cannot prosper and be sustainable, either nationally or globally.

## Notes

1. A warped interpretation of the word 'global' is often implied in much of the discussion. In actual fact, references to developing countries effectively refer to the 12 to 20 systemically significant 'emerging markets'. This is understandable: the new rules apply to economies wishing to participate in the global financial markets. But every country, including those currently by-passed by developments in the markets, is a potential participant in the future. Besides, everyone, including the poor countries, sectors, and groups, has a stake in such an order. Chaos or an unmitigated crisis in the global financial system would have ripple effects not only in the industrial countries but potentially even more so in the poor developing countries which depend on the global system for sourcing investable funds and markets. The key issue is that the manner of achieving the order might affect different members of the community differently, depending on the rules enforced and the individual circumstances. Furthermore, the governance structure of such an institution and its rules are not free from politics. What you have at the end depends on the major actors and main interests represented in the design and operation of the system. Vital interests of poor countries ignored in the process could disadvantage the poor countries and poor people.

2. Communiqué of the Interim Committee of the Board of Governors of the International Monetary Fund, Washington, D.C., April 27, 1999.

3. IMF, 'A Guide to Progress in Strengthening the Architecture of the International Financial System', Washington, D.C., April 28, 1999.

4. The original title of this subsection used by G-22 was 'Transparency and Accountability'.

5. IMF, 'A Guide to Progress...'

6. Particularly in the last two decades, the dominance of one model or the other has largely depended on the waves of political cycles in the dominant economies. It is no accident that the pre-eminence of the neoclassical economics and drive to mono-economics had its debut when the right-of-centre governments emerged in major economies in late 1970s to early 1980s—Reagan in the U.S., Thatcher in the U.K.; Kohl in Germany, etc. Since the mid-1990s, left-of-centre governments have swept

back into power in the U.S., U.K, France, Germany, etc, and it is little surprise that 'social programs' and 'role of the state' are being rediscovered in the policy community. It may be no accident that Joseph Stiglitz, a major exponent of market failures, was the Chief Economist of the World Bank under President Clinton, and there is so much talk about going beyond the neoclassical principles embodied under the 'Washington Consensus'.

7. We refer to these as the 'six half-truths' of the neoclassical view of the global economy. Half-truths because these principles are true only to a very limited extent. If only all (actual) economies operated as the textbook economics describes them, these principles could have greater predictive power.

8. What befell South Korea and any other developing country that sought assistance from Washington is the irony of failure in life. Once you fail in anything visible, then all the things you have done in the past must be 'wrong'. South Korea grew spectacularly rich by doing all the 'wrong' things—close links between government and the *chaebols*, credit subsidies, investment guarantees, protected domestic markets, restrictions on inward FDI, domestic-content requirements, public enterprises, mild financial repression. These were features of the Korean model alongside outward orientation, conservative fiscal policies, and an emphasis on education. Once the financial crisis ensued, the celebrated model of government-business relationship that saw Korea to its greatness became 'crony capitalism', etc.

9. It might sound sarcastic, but from the intrusive nature of the reforms recommended to South Korea (only some one and half pages of macroeconomic issues and about 12 pages of unbelievable details of structural and institutional reforms with more than 80 conditionalities), there is likely to be no limit to what the reforms should be all about. For example, one should not be surprised to see a country being told in the future that the reason why it is in crisis is because the labor force wastes too much time in the mosques on Fridays instead of working. This attitude of 'do it my way' because it is the most 'efficient' is not warranted and likely to backfire.

10. Perhaps one day, the French or the Nordic countries might need the assistance of the IMF. It remains to be seen whether they would be asked to dismantle their welfare systems as a 'conditionality' and reform all their institutions to satisfy the interests of Wall Street and Washington. The Chinese have consistently waged a continuing battle just to be left alone to be Chinese, and evolve their own brand of political governance and market economy.

11. See Annex 1 for a detailed discussion of the conceptual and methodological issues involved in attempting to draw valid inferences.

12. IMF, *International Capital Markets: Developments, Prospects, and Key Policy Issues*, Washington, D.C., September 1999.

13. For some analysts, most of the developing countries under adjustment operated what Thandika Mkandawire calls 'choiceless democracies'. This was a situation where elected parliaments had to wait for their national budgets to be approved by the Bretton Woods institutions and then they perform the formal ceremony of 'approving' the budget. This was a democracy in which the people had 'no choice'.

14. Devesh Kapur, 'The International Monetary Fund: A Cure or A Curse?' in *Foreign Policy*, Summer 1998.

15. This is understandable given the old adage that 'what is good for General Motors is good for America'.

16. Under the current system the poor borrowing countries are defrauded twice. Official lenders, especially the multilateral institutions, have flexed their muscle and wrecked whole economies. A decade or two after the havoc, the institutions turn around and in a cavalier manner simply admit: 'we made some mistakes', 'development is a learning process', 'adjustment alone is not enough to usher in development', and 'there is need to go beyond SAP'. But these were exactly the same things about which the poor countries complained and protested at the beginning but the policies were rammed down their throats taking advantage of the difficult financial predicaments of the countries. Thus, a decade or two later, after inflicting unspeakable human and economic toll, the institutions responsible for the policies get away saying they were wrong without any penalties for their mistakes. On the other hand, the poor countries are held responsible for repaying the loans, which were used to leverage the failed policies and programs. Something is fundamentally wrong with the current system. Even medical doctors get sued for 'malpractice'.

17. Bryant (1999) corroborates this point, and argues for pragmatic incrementalism as the model for reforming the architecture. Such incrementalism should be underpinned by at least seven principles as follows: i) responsibility for improved standards and prudential oversight must begin and end at home; ii) standards and oversight at the world level should take the form of 'core principles' rather than detailed 'codes' or fully specified regulations; iii) the preferred approach at the world level is an encouragement of *agreed minimum standards* combined with the presumption of mutual recognition; iv) when possible, world standards and oversight should rely on market incentives rather than direct restrictions; v) world standards and oversight should highlight disclosure and transparency; vi) monitoring and enforcement of world standards and oversight will eventually be at least as important as sound design; vi) improvements are especially needed in emerging-markets and developing nations, but the advanced industrial nations need to make improvements too.

18. The methodological problems are immense and it is not surprising that valid inferences are sorely lacking. As the UN (1996:21) agrees, 'Current understanding is

limited regarding the nature and relative strengths of the transmission channels and linkages that determine the effects of globalization and outward-oriented liberalization on poverty. The task is made more complicated by the need to consider the immense diversity of local circumstances, the variations of the globalization and liberalization processes and their economic and social effects over time. It is therefore recommended that further research be carried out on this subject'.

19. It is important to distinguish between the effects of the globalization of finance from the effects of financial volatility since they do not necessarily have to go together. Indeed, much of the current proposals are designed to curb instability while deepening financial integration. Would the elimination 'volatility' automatically turn financial globalization into a win-win process?

20. Harris, 1998, presents eight skeptical theses against the claims of globalization. He examines the quantities of international flows and assets as well as price data to investigate whether the law of one price holds. According to him, 'the conclusion they lead to is that the world does not have a globalized economy. At most there is a degree of fractured globalization.' 'Home bias' is still dominant in both investment and financial markets and asset holding, while regional blocks dominate in FDI and trade.

## References

Baker, D., Epstein, G. and Pollin, R., eds., 1998, *Globalization and Progressive Economic Policy*, Cambridge: Cambridge University Press.

Birdsall, N., 1999, 'Globalization and the Developing Countries: The Inequality Risk', ODC, *The New Global Economy and Developing Countries*.

Blackden, C.M., and Bhanu, C., 1999, *Gender, Growth, and Poverty Reduction: Special Program of Assistance for Africa, 1998—Status Report on Poverty in Sub-Saharan Africa*, Washington DC: World Bank.

Blecker, R.A., 1999, *Taming Global Finance: A Better Architecture for Growth and Equity*, Washington DC: Economic Policy Institute.

Bryant, R. C., 1999, 'Standards and Prudential Oversight for an Integrating World Financial System'. Paper prepared for the October 1999 Meeting of the Tokyo Club Foundation for Global Studies, London.

Camdessus, M., 1999a, 'International Financial Policy in the Context of Globalization'. Remarks at the Konrad Adenauer Foundation, Frankfurt, Germany: October 11.

Camdessus, M., 1999b, 'Strengthening the Link Between Economic and Social Policies Within the Framework of a Globalized Economy': Remarks to the Confederal Board of the World Confederation of Labor, Washington DC, October 26.

**57**

Caprio, G., 1999, Presentation at the IMF Forum on 'Getting It Right: Sequencing Financial Sector Reforms', Washington DC, July 15.

Deacon, B., 1999, 'The Social Impact of Globalization on Developed Economies', mimeo.

Demery, L. and Walton, M., 1998, *Are Poverty Reduction and Other 21st Century Social Goals Attainable?* Washington, DC: The World Bank.

Demery, L., Ferroni, M., Grootaert, C. and Vande-Valle, J., 1993, *Understanding the Social Effects of Policy Reform*, Washington DC: The World Bank.

Dooley, M.P., 1998, 'The Tobin Tax: Good Theory, Weak Evidence, Questionable Policy' in M. ul Haq, I. Kaul and I. Grunberg, eds., *The Tobin Tax,* New York: Oxford University Press.

Eichengreen, B., 1999, *Towards a New International Financial Architecture: A Practical Post-Asia Agenda*, Washington DC: Institute for International Economics.

Elbadawi, I.A. and Helleiner, G., 1998, 'African Development in the Context of New World Trade and Financial Regimes: The Role of the WTO and Its Relationship to the World Bank and the IMF'. Paper prepared for the project on 'Africa and New World Trading System', AERC, Nairobi.

Feldstein, M., 1998, 'Refocusing the IMF', *Foreign Affairs*, March/April.

Finger, J.M. and Schuler, P., 1999, 'Implementation of Uruguay Round Commitments: The Development Challenge', mimeo, The World Bank.

Griffith-Jones, S., Ocampo, J.A. and Cailloux, J., 1999, 'Proposals for a New International Architecture, with Special Emphasis on Needs of Poorer Countries', mimeo.

Harris, L., 1998, 'The Dynamics of Globalization: Eight Skeptical Theses'. Paper presented at the UNU/AERC joint conference on Africa-Asia Comparative Development Experience, Tokyo (August, 2-3).

Kanbur, R. and Lustig, N., 1999, 'Why is Inequality Back on the Agenda', Inter-American Development Bank.

Lee, Eddy, 1998, *The Asian Financial Crisis: The Challenge for Social Policy*, Geneva: ILO.

OECD, 1998, *Open Markets Matter: The Benefits of Trade and Investment Liberalisation*, Paris: OECD.

Polanyi, K., 1944, *The Great Transformation*, Boston: Beacon Press.

Reinicke, W.H., 1998, *Global Public Policy: Governing without Government?* Washington DC: The Brookings Institution.

Rodrik, D., 1999a, 'Governing the Global Economy: Does One Architecture Style Fit All'. Paper prepared for the Brookings Institution Trade Policy Forum conference on Governing in a Global Economy, April 15-16.

Rodrik, D., 1999b, 'How Far Will International Economic Integration Go?'. Prepared for the Millennium issue of the *Journal of Economic Perspectives*, to be published in early 2000.

Rodrik, D., 1999c, 'Rethinking the World Economy', mimeo.

Rodrik, D., 1999d, *The New Global Economy and Developing Countries: Making Openness Work*, Washington, DC: Overseas Development Council.

Rodrik, D., 1998, 'Who needs capital-account convertibility?', Harvard University. Paper written as contribution to a symposium edited by Peter Kenen (to be published as part of a 'Princeton Essay in International Finance').

Rodrik, D., 1997, *Has Globalization Gone Too Far?* Washington DC: Institute for International Economics.

Rubin, R., 1999, 'Restoring Global Financial Stability', Testimony of U.S. Treasury Secretary to the House Committee on Banking and Financial Services, May 20.

Ruminska-Zimny, E., 1999, 'Globalization and Human Development in Transition Economies', mimeo.

Soludo, C.C., 1999, 'Thinking About Potential Social Impacts of the Proposals for a New Financial Architecture'. Paper presented at Oxfam America workshop on International Financial Institutions, Annapolis, May 12.

Stewart, F., 1998, 'Adjustment and Poverty in Asia: Old Solutions and New Problems', Working Paper Number 20. QEH Working Paper Series.

Stiglitz, J., 1998a, 'The Role of International Financial Institutions in the Current Global Economy', Address to the Chicago Council of Foreign Relations, February 27.

Stiglitz, J., 1998b, 'Towards a New Paradigm for Development: Strategies, Policies, and Processes'. Paper presented as the 1998 Prebisch Lecture at UNCTAD, Geneva. October, 19.

UN, 1996, *Globalization and Liberalization: Effects of International Economic Relations on Poverty*, New York: Inter-Agency Thematic Contribution to the International Year for the Eradication of Poverty.

UNCTAD, 1998, *Trade and Development Report: Financial Instability, Growth in Africa*, Geneva: United Nations.

UNDP, 1999, *Human Development Report*, New York.

UNDP, 1998, *Overcoming Human Poverty*, New York.

UNICEF, 1990, *State of the World's Children 1990*, Oxford: Oxford University Press.

Volcker, P., 1998, 'Emerging Economies in a Sea of Global Finance', Charles Rostov Lecture, SAIS, Johns Hopkins University, Washington DC, April, 9.

Wiseman, J., ed., 1997, *Alternatives to Globalisation: An Asia-Pacific Perspective*, Australia, Community Aid Abroad.

Wolfensohn, J., 1999, 'A Proposal for a Comprehensive Development Framework'. Memo to the Board, management and staff of the World Bank group.

## Appendix Table 1
## Net Flow of Resources 1992–1997
### (Annual averages, in billion dollars and percentages)

| | Direct Foreign Investment | | Portfolio Equity Flows | | Grants | | Bilateral Financing | | Multilateral Financing (excluding IMF) | |
|---|---|---|---|---|---|---|---|---|---|---|
| | Amount | % | Amount | % | Amount | % | Amount | % | Amount | % |
| Developin countries | 99.0 | 100.0 | 35.7 | 100.0 | 29.7 | 100.0 | 2.9 | 100.0 | 13.7 | 100.0 |
| Excluding China | 66.8 | 67.5 | 31.7 | 88.9 | 29.4 | 99.0 | 0.5 | 19.0 | 11.6 | 84.5 |
| **Low Income Countries** | 6.7 | 6.8 | 3.4 | 9.5 | 15.8 | 53.2 | 0.8 | 27.1 | 5.9 | 43.4 |
| India | 1.6 | 1.6 | 2.5 | 6.9 | 0.6 | 1.9 | -0.3 | -11.3 | 1.0 | 7.4 |
| Other Countries | 5.1 | 5.2 | 0.9 | 2.6 | 15.2 | 51.3 | 1.1 | 38.4 | 4.9 | 36.0 |
| China a/ | 32.1 | 32.5 | 3.9 | 11.1 | 0.3 | 1.0 | 2.3 | 81.0 | 2.1 | 15.5 |
| **Middle Income Countries** | 60.1 | 60.8 | 28.3 | 79.4 | 13.7 | 46.1 | -0.2 | -8.1 | 5.6 | 41.1 |
| Argentina | 4.4 | 4.5 | 1.7 | 4.9 | 0.0 | 0.1 | -0.1 | -3.2 | 0.9 | 6.6 |
| Brazil | 7.7 | 7.7 | 4.1 | 11.5 | 0.1 | 0.2 | -1.3 | -43.4 | -0.1 | -0.6 |
| Russian Federation | 1.9 | 1.9 | 1.1 | 3.1 | 1.1 | 3.7 | 0.6 | 21.4 | 0.9 | 6.2 |
| Indonesia | 3.5 | 3.6 | 2.4 | 6.8 | 0.2 | 0.8 | 1.2 | 41.7 | 0.1 | 0.9 |
| Korea Republic b/ | 1.5 | 1.5 | 3.1 | 8.8 | 0.0 | 0.0 | -0.2 | -5.4 | 0.6 | 4.1 |
| Mexico | 8.1 | 8.2 | 5.1 | 14.3 | 0.0 | 0.1 | -0.6 | -21.4 | 0.3 | 2.2 |
| Other Countries | 33.0 | 33.2 | 10.7 | 30.1 | 12.2 | 41.2 | 0.1 | 2.2 | 3.0 | 21.7 |

| | Bonds | | Commercial Loans | | Other Loans | | Total | | Memo GDP | Popu. |
|---|---|---|---|---|---|---|---|---|---|---|
| | Amount | % | Amount | % | Amount | % | Amount | % | Amount | % |
| **Developing Countries** | 34.6 | 100.0 | 28.3 | 100.0 | 4.9 | 100.0 | 248.7 | 100.0 | 100.0 | 00.0 |
| Excluding China | 32.9 | 95.2 | 26.6 | 94.0 | 1.1 | 21.4 | 200.7 | 80.7 | 89.2 | 74.8 |
| **Low Income Countries** | 0.5 | 1.5 | 0.9 | 3.3 | 0.4 | 7.2 | 34.5 | 13.9 | 11.4 | 41.0 |
| India | 0.4 | 1.1 | 0.8 | 2.8 | 0.4 | 8.9 | 6.9 | 2.8 | 5.6 | 19.3 |
| Other Countries | 0.2 | 0.4 | 0.2 | 0.6 | -0.1 | -1.7 | 27.6 | 11.1 | 5.8 | 21.7 |
| China a/ | 1.7 | 4.8 | 1.7 | 6.0 | 3.9 | 78.6 | 48.0 | 19.3 | 10.8 | 25.2 |
| **Middle Income Countries** | 32.4 | 93.7 | 25.7 | 90.7 | 0.7 | 14.2 | 166.3 | 66.9 | 77.8 | 33.9 |
| Argentina | 5.5 | 15.9 | 0.8 | 2.9 | 0.0 | -0.9 | 13.3 | 5.3 | 5.0 | 0.7 |
| Brazil | 3.1 | 9.0 | 8.2 | 29.0 | -0.6 | -11.3 | 21.2 | 8.5 | 10.5 | 3.3 |
| Russian Federation | 0.8 | 2.2 | 0.3 | 1.1 | 1.4 | 28.7 | 8.1 | 3.2 | 7.3 | 3.1 |
| Indonesia | 1.6 | 4.7 | 0.9 | 3.2 | 0.2 | 3.7 | 10.2 | 4.1 | 3.4 | 4.0 |
| Korea Republic b/ | 4.5 | 12.9 | 4.1 | 14.5 | -0.2 | -4.8 | 13.4 | 5.4 | 7.3 | 0.9 |
| Mexico | 5.2 | 15.2 | 0.3 | 1.1 | -0.3 | -6.9 | 18.2 | 7.3 | 6.7 | 1.9 |
| Other Countries | 11.7 | 33.8 | 11.0 | 38.9 | 0.3 | 5.6 | 81.9 | 32.9 | 37.6 | 19.8 |

**Sources**: The World Bank, *Global Development Finance*, 1999, Washington DC, March 1999; and World Economic Indicator, Washington, DC, 1998 for GDP and population data.

a/ The World Bank considered China as a low income country until 1998. Since 1999 it is included as a middle income country. In this Table it is considered under a separate category.

b/ The World Bank considers Korea as a high income country, but it is included as a middle income country in the Global Development Finance, 1999.

## Appendix Table 2
## Private Financial Flows to Low Income Countries (in $ billions)

|  | 1995 | 1996 | 1997 | 1998 |
|---|---|---|---|---|
| **Net Private Capital Flows** | | | | |
| **Low Income Countries**[1] | 11.3 | 14.6 | 17.0 | 15.2 |
| Africa | 6.8 | 7.6 | 16.3 | na |
| Sub-Sahara Africa[2] | 9.7 | 4.4 | 8.1 | na |
| South Africa[3] | 8.3 | 5.9 | 13.3 | 9.9 |
| India[4] | 5.1 | 16.8 | 15.1 | 6.6 |
| Pakistan | 2.6 | 3.7 | 1.3 | na |
| | | | | |
| **Net Direct Investment** | | | | |
| **Low Income Countries**[1] | 7.3 | 9.3 | 10.6 | 10.6 |
| Africa | 4.2 | 5.5 | 7.6 | 6.8 |
| South Africa[3] | 1.0 | 0.8 | 1.7 | 0.5 |
| India[4] | 2.1 | 2.4 | 3.3 | 1.6 |
| Pakistan | 0.7 | 0.9 | 0.7 | na |
| | | | | |
| **Net Portfolio Investment** | | | | |
| **Low Income Countries**[1] | 3.0 | 5.9 | 4.7 | 0 |
| *Of which Banks* | 0.3 | 0.2 | 2.3 | -0.4 |
| *Equities* | 2.7 | 5.7 | 2.4 | 0.4 |
| Africa | 1.5 | -0.2 | 2.9 | 3.5 |
| South Africa[3] | 3.1 | 3.0 | 12.8 | 10.7 |
| India[4] | 1.6 | 4.0 | 2.5 | -0.3 |
| Pakistan | na | 0.3 | 0.4 | na |
| | | | | |
| **Other Net Investment** | | | | |
| **Low Income Countries**[1] | 1.0 | -0.6 | 1.7 | 4.7 |
| Africa | 1.2 | 2.3 | 5.8 | na |
| South Africa[3] | 4.2 | 2.1 | -1.2 | -1.3 |
| India[4] | 1.4 | 10.4 | 9.3 | 5.3 |
| Pakistan | 1.9 | 2.5 | 1.2 | na |

**Sources**: WEO, 1999, CMDC, 1998, Global Development Finance, 1999, International Finance Statistics, 1999.

1: Global Development Finance, 1999

2: These data comes from CMDC and are not necessary comparable.

3. First three quarters of 1998

4: First two quarters of 1998

5: Mainly loans.

**Appendix Table 3**
**Changes in Prices of Selected Products (per cent)**

| Products | 6/97 – 4/98 | 5/98 – 12/98 | Products | 6/97 – 4/98 | 5/98 – 12/98 |
|---|---|---|---|---|---|
| Tropical Beverages | -19.3 | -11.6 | Cotton | -14.6 | -2.7 |
| Sugar | -17.7 | -12.5 | Copper | -31.1 | -15.0 |
| Wheat | -10.1 | -1.5 | Nickel | -23.6 | -22.7 |
| Maize | -9.3 | -7.1 | Zinc | -19.0 | -9.6 |
| Rubber | -32.9 | -16.1 | Lead | -7.0 | -7.8 |
| Tropical Sawnwood | -32.7 | +3.2 | Aluminium | -9.5 | -8.5 |
| Wood | -14.6 | -2.7 | Crude Oil | -24.6 | -25.9 |

**Source**: TDR, 1998 and Monthly Commodity Price Bulletin (MCPB), 1999.

**Appendix Table 4**
**Changes in Terms of Trade for Africa and Latin America (per cent)**

| | 1990-94[1] | 1995-97[1] | 1996 | 1997 | 1998 | 1999 | 2000 |
|---|---|---|---|---|---|---|---|
| Sub-Saharan Africa | -1.3 | 1.9 | 5.0 | -0.6 | -9.1 | -2.5 | 3.6 |
| Oil Exporters | -2.6 | 7.7 | 22.6 | 1.9 | -28.8 | -10.4 | 16.5 |
| Non-fuel Exporters | -0.4 | 0.1 | -1.1 | -0.3 | -1.3 | -0.1 | -0.5 |
| Latin America and Caribbean | na | na | -0.9 | 3.8 | - | na | na |

**Sources**: WEO, 1999, ECLAC, 1998c.

(1) Average

\* Estimate, na: not available

**Appendix Table 5**
Poverty Trends in Developing and Transitional Economies
1987–1993
(People below poverty line of US$1 per capita per day)

| Region | Coverage* %  | Number of Poor (millions) | | | Headcount Index (%) | | | Poverty Gap (%) | | |
|---|---|---|---|---|---|---|---|---|---|---|
| | | 1987 | 1990 | 1993 | 1987 | 1990 | 1993 | 1987 | 1990 | 1993 |
| East Asia & the Pacific | 88.0 | 464.0 | 468.2 | 445.8 | 28.2 | 28.5 | 26.0 | 8.3 | 8.0 | 7.8 |
| (excluding China) | (61.5) | (109.2) | (89.3) | (73.5) | (23.2) | (17.6) | 13.7) | (3.8) | (3.1) | (3.1) |
| Eastern Europe & Central Asia | 85.9 | 2.2 | na | 14.5 | 0.6 | na | 3.5 | 0.2 | na | 1.1 |
| Latin America & the Caribbean | 83.9 | 91.2 | 101.0 | 109.6 | 22.0 | 23.0 | 23.5 | 8.2 | 9.0 | 9.1 |
| Middle East & North Africa | 46.7 | 10.3 | 10.4 | 10.7 | 4.7 | 4.3 | 4.1 | 0.9 | 0.7 | 0.6 |
| South Asia | 98.4 | 479.9 | 480.4 | 514.7 | 45.4 | 43.0 | 43.1 | 14.1 | 12.3 | 12.6 |
| Sub-Saharan Africa | 65.9 | 179.6 | 201.2 | 218.6 | 38.5 | 39.3 | 39.1 | 14.4 | 14.5 | 15.3 |
| **Total** | **85.0** | **122.7** | **na** | **131.4** | **30.1** | **na** | **29.4** | **9.5** | **na** | **9.2** |
| Total (excluding Eastern Europe & Central Asia) | 85.0 | 122.5 | 126.1 | 129.9 | 33.3 | 32.9 | 31.8 | 10.8 | 10.3 | 10.5 |

**Source**: World Bank (1996a).

\* Percentage of population covered by at least one survey.

## Annex 1: Conceptual and Methodological Issues in
## Evaluating Impacts of the NGFA

As evident from the elements of the NGFA summarized in Chapter II, the Architecture aims to provide a public good—a global governance system to ensure order and stability of the financial system as part of the globalization structure. As with every public good, there are both positive and negative externalities, and there are winners and losers. In some cases, the winners and losers may not necessarily be distinct groups of agents as an agent could both gain and lose from the architecture. Some might however be outright winners or losers. Therefore, any impact assessment would have to focus on the *net effects*.

The potential impacts are many and varied but a narrower focus on the social sector would at least evaluate the impacts on real income including its growth and distribution within and across countries, relative prices, (re)allocation of government expenditures in favour or against social spending, primary health care and education, gender differentiated effects, urbanization, crime, and the environment. Impacts on specific target groups such as the poor, women, and smallholders also need to be evaluated. To evaluate such impacts, it is necessary to clearly identify the major channels of transmission of effects of the NGFA. In the context of the proposals in the NGFA, these could include: global financial transfers (portfolio/equity ownership and location, ODA, FDI, and capital flight); government budgetary (re)allocations to meet increased responsibilities; alteration of relative prices and the consequent household and target group responses; trade and investment flows; and public goods nature of proposals including stability of the global system and potential growth dividend.

A neat accounting of these effects is not easy, and not surprisingly much of the literature is adorned with extreme conjectures.[18] Take two examples. At one end is a view eloquently captured by some NGOs in a paper entitled 'A Call to Action...' (p.1) as follows: 'Financial volatility is bringing massive economic breakdown, insecurity, increased poverty, unemployment and dislocation, assaults on environmental and labor conditions, loss of wilderness and biodiversity, massive population shifts, increased ethnic and racial tensions, and international conflict'. Implicitly, financial volatility is assumed to be the consequence of globalization. On the other hand, the disparate views in the compendium by the UN (1996:9-11) still lead them to conclude that:

Greater openness of the financial sector has encouraged increased portfolio investment flows into a number of middle-income countries, which has helped ease their foreign exchange constraint, augmented the marginal efficiency of capital in the countries concerned, and encouraged economic discipline while punishing policy failure. By contributing to the appreciation of the real exchange rate, such inflows have also helped to dampen inflation... While most developing countries will gain from the globalization process, some will benefit more than others, and a number of countries with initial conditions that make them less suited to take advantage of globalization will lose out and become more marginalized in relation to other countries. However, it is expected that total benefits for the developing countries as a whole will be greater than total costs, and that absolute poverty will as a result decline in global terms.[19]

The two examples illustrate both the potentials and the dangers in drawing inferences. The potential is that there is a rich menu of potential effects that can be established. The danger is that literally everything can be attributed to the process. The critics have a tendency to blame globalization or the financial crises for all the woes of the global economy or of individual countries and groups within them. Alternatively, the adherents assemble massive evidence on how the global economy has improved over the last three decades (especially the fortunes of the developing countries) and ascribe all the benefits to globalization and financial integration. This way of couching the debate leads to acrimonious and often bloated claims that cannot be substantiated.

Substantiation is extremely difficult and existing inferences are at best conjectural and controversial principally because of the weaknesses of the methodology. Four key methodological problems confront attempts to make definitive inferences and they include: pertinent and consistent data on the units of analysis across and within countries; problems of attribution (cause-and-effect relationships); relevant counterfactuals; problems of aggregation and the transition between micro-macro level analyses.

The first methodological difficulty is that of correctly isolating the potential effects of the NGFA from other variables. The problem is at two levels. First, the proposals consist of a group of instruments, some of which could have contradictory impacts on the social sectors. Second, these proposals would be implemented in an environment already overloaded with a multiplicity of reforms (such as the SAPs in most developing countries). How do we know which effects are due to the proposed NGFA and which due to other reforms and shocks buffeting the economies? The problem of attribution (isolating cause-and-effect relationships) is all the more problematic in evaluating the potential impacts of the new proposals. Here, we are dealing with a prospective event (new financial architecture) and the inferences are based upon some 'simulations' of possible outcomes. In such simulations, the baseline is often not revealed, and this makes it difficult to determine the 'marginal' impacts of the proposals. Without a clearly defined baseline, it is extremely difficult to simulate consequences of sets of policies let alone isolating the marginal effects of and individual policy.

To illustrate the problem of a valid baseline, let us make two assumptions regarding the frame of analysis. Let us assume that the NGFA simply strengthens and deepens an existing structure—the globalization process. In this case, the existing historical data can be attributed to this process. Thus, if we use the existing data as the best predictor of the counterfactual of what would happen without the NGFA, any potential changes can then be attributed to the new architecture. To draw inference, it boils down to the question of whether they would gain or lose from the current system as compared to the new system incorporating the proposed changes. On this premise, historical data can be of help and can constitute an essential baseline. Our job is simply to infer the 'marginal' changes due to the improvements or deepening of the structure.

There is another facet of the counterfactual. Some analysts believe that globalization is not a costless exercise. If the baseline shows a tendency towards inequities, instabilities, etc., a fundamental question is how much of these should be attributed to the globalization process of increased interaction and integration of national economies, and how much to the natural attributes of the capitalist system? Some analysts might argue that the free market economic system is inherently inequitable and much of its dynamism stems from this feature. Without deeper integration, would the global system and relationships within countries have been less inequitable within and across countries? This is a critical question even if one believes that the database for the past three decades constitutes a robust baseline.

An alternative framework is that presented by those who dispute that globalization (deeper integration) has occurred to the extent that outcomes in the global economy and within countries can be attributed to it. They argue that the extent of globalization is being exaggerated, and much of the outcomes within and across countries are still products of differences in initial conditions, geographic location, and domestic policy choices (Harris 1998; Rodrik 1997, 1999b, c, d, etc.).[20] Under this scenario, it is even more difficult to know what to attribute to globalization.

Beside the problems of disentangling cause-and-effect relationships and appropriate counterfactuals, a daunting problem of any analysis is the paucity of consistent and reliable data. The analysis of social impacts has both vertical and horizontal dimensions. The vertical is the inter-country comparisons of the differential impacts on the rich and poor countries, while the horizontal analysis evaluates the differential impacts on the rich and poor agents within countries. In both levels of analysis, there are problems of micro-meso-macro linkages.

The inter-country differentials involving mostly the use of time-series analysis of trends in broad macro aggregates such as capital/financial flows, trade, investment, incidence and severity of poverty, income growth and dispersion, etc., are much easier to analyse than the micro-meso level linkages. The problem of disentangling cause-and-effect still remains.

The within country (target group) analysis is a lot more difficult especially in the context of inadequate data, country-specific nature of the analysis, and target group orientation. Proposals for NGFA are supposed to affect market prices and the social and economic infrastructure, which in turn affect household or target group behaviour. How the target groups (poor, women, smallholders, etc.) modify their income-earning activities, consumption behaviour, and satisfaction of basic needs depend on the impacts of the NGFA proposals on the labor markets, credit and product markets, health and educational services, and the state of economic infrastructure such as transportation and irrigation. The analysis here is generally of the macro-micro linkages. This two stage approach should produce results for the potential changes in income distribution, poverty, feminisation of labor force, occupational shifts, asset ownership and relative performance of those with and without financial assets. Such an analysis would require consistent panel data over time.

Sub-Saharan Africa is most notorious for the paucity of reliable data for evaluating the meso-micro linkages and social impacts. Efforts to remedy the situation are very recent and not comprehensive enough for the kinds of analysis warranted by NGFA evaluation. Data now exist (compiled for the UNDP's Human Development Reports and compiled by the World Bank) to make broad statements about the social conditions in Africa. Such statements about the status at a point in time, is very different from drawing inferences about causal linkages. The same problem has hamstrung effective evaluation of the social impacts of SAPs. In the OECD economies, there might be more consistent data, but the difficulty of attribution is not diminished.

**67**

**Annex 2:** World Summit for Social Development Goals and Targets
(Quantitative and time-bound goals and targets adopted in Copenhagen, March 1995)

| | By Year |
|---|---|
| **1. Poverty Eradication Policies and Strategies** | |
| Formulate or strengthen as a matter of urgency, and preferably 1996 or by the year 1996, national policies and strategies geared to substantially reducing overall poverty in the shortest possible time, reducing inequalities and eradicating absolute poverty by a target date to be specified by each country in its national context. | 1996 or thereafter |
| **2. Education** | |
| a) Universal access to basic education 2000 | 2000 |
| b) Completion of primary education by at least 80 per cent of primary school-age children 2000 | 2000 |
| c) Closing of the gender gap in primary and secondary school education | 2005 |
| d) Universal primary education | 2015 |
| **3. Health** | |
| a) Life expectancy of not less than 60 years | 2000 |
| b) Reduction of mortality rates of infants and children under five of age by one third of the 1990 level or 50 to 70 per 1,000 live births, whichever is less | 2000 |
| Infant mortality rate below 35 per 1,000 live births and under-five mortality rate below 45 per 1,000 | 2015 |
| c) Reduction of maternal mortality rate to one half of the 1990 rate | 2000 |
| Further reduction of maternal mortality rate to one half of the rate in 2000 | 2015 |
| d) Reduction of severe and moderate malnutrition among children under five years of age by half of the 1990 level | 2000 |
| e) Primary health care for all | 2000 |
| f) Reproductive health to all individuals of appropriate ages | 2015 |
| g) Reduction of malaria mortality and morbidity by at least 20 per cent from their 1995 levels in at least 75 per cent of affected countries | 2000 |
| h) Eradicating, eliminating or controlling major diseases constituting global health problems, in accordance with paragraph 6.12 of Agenda 21 | 2000 |
| **4. Resource Mobilisation and Allocation (20:20 Compact)** | |
| Agreeing on a mutual commitment between interested developed and developing country partners to allocate, on average, 20 per cent of official development assistance (ODA) and 20 per cent of the national budget, respectively, to basic social programs | As soon as possible |

**Source**: United Nations, World Summit for Social Development, Report of the World Summit for Social Development (Copenhagen, 6-12 March 1995), (A/CONF.166/9), 19 April 1995, pages 13, 50, 51.

## Annex 3: OECD/DAC Quality of Life Goals

|  | By Year |
|---|---|

**1. Economic Well-Being or Poverty Reduction**

Proportion of people living in extreme poverty (defined by the World Bank as those with expenditures of less than US$1 per day per capita at 1985 purchasing power parity or PPP) in developing countries to be reduced by at least on half (of the 1994 level of 30 per cent or .3 billion persons) — 2015

**2. Social Development**

**a) Education**

i) Universal primary education in all countries (same as World Summit for Social Development or WSSD target) — 2015

ii) Elimination of gender disparity in primary and secondary education (same as WSSD target) — 2005

**b) Health**

i) Reduction in mortality rate of infants and children under five years of age by two-thirds of the 1990 rate (same as WSSD target) — 2015

ii) Reduction in maternal mortality rate by three-fourths of the 1990 rate (same as WSSD target) — 2015

iii) Access to reproductive health services for all persons of appropriate ages through the primary health-care system (same as WSSD target) — 2015

**3. Environment**

Preparation and implementation of a national strategy for sustainable development in all countries — 2005

**Source**: OECD-DAC, 'Shaping the 21st Century: The Contribution of Development Cooperation', Annex to *Overview of the DAC Chair in 1996 Development Assistance Report*, Paris, pages 19–21.